the
banquet
of life

PETER HOCKEN

the
banquet
of life

the dignity of the human person

Alive Publishing

First published in 2004 by Alive Publishing Ltd.
Graphic House, 124 City Road, Stoke on Trent ST4 2PH
Tel: +44 (0) 1782 745600.   Fax: +44 (0) 1782 745500
www.biblealive.co.uk   e-mail:editor@biblealive.co.uk

©2004 Alive Publishing
British Library Catalogue-in-Publication Data. A catalogue record for
this book is available from the British Library.

ISBN 0-9540335-4-X

Contents

About the author

Monsignor Peter Hocken is a Roman Catholic priest of the Diocese of Northampton and was Chaplain to the Bishop of Northampton and is now resident in Vienna. He holds a Phd in theology from Birmingham University.

Other books by Peter Hocken include:

Available from Alive Publishing:

- *Blazing the Trail - where is the Holy Spirit leading the Church?*
- *God's Masterplan - penetrating the mystery of Christ.*

Available from Paternoster Press:

- *Streams of Renewal - the origins and early development of the Charismatic movement in Great Britain.*

Foreword

by Lord Alton of Liverpool

Occasionally, a book is written on a subject of such importance that I wonder if it should be made compulsory reading! We live in a world where life is increasingly cheap. That is why the Church's teaching on the utter dignity of the human person is a jewel in its crown. Peter Hocken should be congratulated for his discerning reflections. The belief that every person is made in the image of God - and therefore of infinite worth - is a central tenet of Christianity. Throughout history this belief has spiritually nourished Christians and often given them the fortitude to stand against tyranny and to empower the dispossessed.

The Banquet of Life articulates why the inalienable dignity of each human person fundamentally re-orientates our view of the world. This book is a crucial tool for anyone wanting insight on family relations, gaining perspective on work/life balance, cultivating community and understanding the importance of human rights. *The Banquet of Life* has identified a key value around which many of us can and should unite. I thoroughly commend this book to you!

Lord Alton of Liverpool

March 2004

Introduction

Throughout the year 2003, I contributed a series of articles to *Bible Alive* on the theme of the dignity of the human person in the teaching of the Catholic Church. Several readers remarked that this series ought to be published as a book, so that the contents would have a longer life than magazine articles normally enjoy. Hence *The Banquet of Life*. The title is taken from a passage in the encyclical *Sollicitudo rei socialis* of Pope John Paul II: "Solidarity helps us to see the "other" ..... as our "neighbour", a "helper" (Gen 2:18-20), to be made a sharer, on a par with ourselves, in the banquet of life to which all are equally invited by God" (SRS, 39). The banquet of life is an image of human togetherness in joy, expressing a vision of God's gift of the celebration of all that is most human. It provides an excellent title for a summary of official Catholic teaching on the dignity of the human person.

In fact, the resulting book expands on the *Bible Alive* articles in several ways. The tight space limits on the monthly articles left little scope for developing important points in the Church's social teaching. So while the book remains at the level of a popular introduction, some points are here developed in more detail. One of the themes very characteristic of Pope John Paul II, namely that of solidarity, that I had wanted to include in the series, had to be omitted due to insufficient months in the year. It is now the subject of an extra chapter. A slight change has been made in the chapter order, to follow the logic of a book rather than the demands of a magazine following the calendar of the church year.

It was also suggested that this kind of simple introduction to the dignity of the human person would provide an excellent basis for small group discussion. So at the end of each chapter, there is a short list of sources to consult in magisterial teaching, followed by a few questions for discussion.

In line with the objectives of *Bible Alive* and of Alive Publishing, an effort has also been made to show the biblical foundations of Catholic social teaching. It is recommended that discussion groups using the questions provided should reflect together on both contemporary Church teaching and the biblical texts cited.

Peter Hocken

Vienna

January 2004

Chapter 1

Made for Dialogue

One of the most startling changes in the policy, and indeed the teaching, of the Catholic Church at the Second Vatican Council was the decision for dialogue. It is not the custom of the Church to herald even the most significant changes as revolutionary, but in fact the decision for dialogue represents a momentous change in the stance and in the teaching of the Catholic Church.

As with other major advances in the history of the Church, in dialogue there were some pioneering predecessors. One was the Italian Jesuit missionary to China in the late 16th century, Fr Matteo Ricci, who entered into a deep dialogue with Chinese culture and Confucian philosophy. Within Christendom, the Catholic Church had seen herself as the unique depository of divine revelation in a way that made unlikely any authentic human dialogue with critics and with those outside the Church.

The ferocity of the Reformation critique made any move in the direction of dialogue more difficult, a stance that was not overcome until the opening of the "windows of the Church" by Blessed John XXIII. Pope John paved the way to dialogue, above all through his lifestyle which was always open to the goodness and the truth in all those he met.

The adoption of dialogue as the "way of the Church" was closely linked with the theme of the dignity of the human person that has become a major emphasis in Catholic teaching since Vatican Two. Pope John XXIII did not long survive the first session of the Council, but only two months before his death in June 1963, he issued his famous encyclical on peace, *Pacem in terris*. This was the first magisterial document to detail a list of human rights, which were grounded in "man's personal dignity".

At the start of the Council, the focus had been on the inner life of the Church. But many Church leaders felt that the Council must say something about the relationship of the Church to the contemporary world. The lead was taken by Cardinal Léon-Joseph Suenens of Belgium and Cardinal Giovanni Battista Montini of Milan, soon to be elected Pope as the successor of John XXIII, taking the name of Paul VI. Out of their initiative came the establishment of a joint commission to prepare a document on the Church in the modern world. One of the prelates appointed to this commission was Mgr Karol Wojtyla from Cracow, Poland, later to become Pope John Paul II.

The importance of dialogue

However, before the Council finalized the document on the Church in the modern world, Pope Paul VI issued his first encyclical letter, *Ecclesiam suam* (1964). In this letter, Paul VI outlined his vision for the Church and for the Council. *Ecclesiam suam* presents three tasks for the Church: self-awareness, renewal and dialogue. A greater self-awareness of the Church, both of her riches and of her needs, leads to renewal. Renewal then requires and leads to dialogue.

For Paul VI, dialogue is the way of the Lord. Our God is a God who speaks to his people, and to whom his people speak in prayer. The God of Israel is a God of dialogue. There can be no covenant without dialogue. But it is supremely the Incarnation that shows the depths of divine dialogue. The Son of God enters this world, and dwells among us. Jesus goes out to meet the weak, the sick, the needy, the suffering and the sinful. His encounter with the woman of Samaria at Jacob's well reveals the extraordinary character of this divine-human dialogue that is a profound meeting, full of respect, equal and yet unequal. He who is the well of life says to a foreign woman: "Give me a drink" (John 4:7). Jesus initiates the dialogue. He speaks to the woman where she is, without condescension, yet in full honesty. He knows her sin, but he respects her dignity. He speaks words of life that come from the depths of God. These words open up a dialogue of salvation.

We are to follow the example of the Lord. "God Himself took the initiative in the dialogue of salvation. 'He has first loved us' (1 John 4:10). We, therefore, must be the first to ask for a dialogue with men, without waiting to be summoned to it by others" (ES, 72). Jesus died for all on the cross. He invites all to the banquet of eternal life. "The dialogue of salvation was made accessible to all. It applied to everyone without distinction. Hence our dialogue too should be as universal as we can make it. That is to say, it must be catholic" (ES, 76). Jesus did not restrict his conversation to those who considered themselves righteous or who had impressive human credentials. "The dialogue of salvation did not depend on the merits of those with whom it was initiated, nor on the results it would be likely to achieve. 'Those who are well have no need of a physician' (Luke 5:31). Neither, therefore, should we set limits to our dialogue or seek in it our own advantage" (ES, 74). As Christians we enter dialogue with the intentions and the motivation of Jesus himself. "The dialogue of salvation sprang from the goodness and the love of God. 'God so loved the world that he gave his only Son' (John 3:16). Our inducement, therefore, to enter into this dialogue must be nothing other than a love which is ardent and sincere" (ES, 73).

The Church's conversion to dialogue is part of a deeper conformity to Christ. Human beings are made for God, and we are made for dialogue. That is to say, we are created to talk and communicate with God and with one another. Respectful relationships and salvation can never ultimately be separated

4

from one another. The decision for dialogue is not an abandonment of missionary work. But we approach others in a much humbler and more respectful spirit. As John Paul II has said: "This missionary duty, moreover, does not prevent us from approaching dialogue with an attitude of profound willingness to listen" (NMI, 56).

Four concentric circles

Paul VI expressed his vision of dialogue with four concentric circles (ES, 96 and following). This picture is still helpful for us today in understanding the stance of the Catholic Church. First circle: All Humanity without exception. Second circle: Non-Christian Religions. Third circle: Other Christians. Fourth circle: Catholics. Dialogue is needed with all. But it takes different forms with the different groupings.

For those without any religion and indifferent to the question of God, we need first to understand their inner attitudes. Paul VI wrote of the pastoral need "to understand the reasons for his [the modern atheist's] mental turmoil and his denial of God" (ES, 104). A fuller attempt to understand atheism and its challenge was made in the council document, *Gaudium et spes*. The Church "tries ... to seek out the secret motives which lead the atheistic mind to deny God" (GS, 21). It seems clear that Archbishop Wojtyla contributed significantly to this discussion. The council recognized that Christians bear a responsibility for the rise of atheism. We can present a distorted and thus false picture of God, that causes others to reject belief in God. In this way we "conceal rather than ... reveal the true nature of God and of religion" (GS, 19).

Our attitudes to adherents of non-Christian religions, particularly to Muslims, have become more crucial since September 11th, 2001. The threat from terrorism has reminded us of how easily religious sentiment can be inflamed and harnessed to destructive purposes. But the Catholic Church calls us to honest and respectful relationships grounded in dialogue. Here Paul VI said of the Muslims: "We do well to admire these people for all that is good and true in their worship of God" (ES, 107). While we cannot regard all the non-Christian religions as being "on an equal footing" (ES, 107), "we desire to join with them in promoting and defending common ideals in the spheres of religious liberty, human brotherhood, education, culture, social welfare, and civic order" (ES, 108).

Paul VI introduced the third circle of other Christians outside the Catholic communion as "the circle which is nearest to us" (ES, 109). During the centuries of Christendom, the nearest had been the furthest, as other Christians were treated and, where possible, punished as heretics. Blessed John XXIII was the first Pope to recognize that what unites Catholics to other Christians is greater than what divides. For what unites is the indwelling of the Holy Spirit, the confession of Jesus as Lord and Saviour, the recognition of God as Father and Creator of all. The points that divide us still cannot be on the same level.

The relationship of the Catholic Church to the Orthodox and Protestant churches and communities is now rooted in dialogue. After nearly forty years, we are seeing some of the fruit. The dialogue method has led, for example, to the Joint Declaration on Justification between the Roman Catholic Church and the Lutheran World Federation (1999). The latest report of the Anglican-Roman Catholic International Commission on "The Gift of Authority" shows how a difficult issue like authority can be better understood in the full biblical context of God's eternal plan being realized through the sending of his Son and of his Spirit.

Dialogue, the human person and Jesus Christ

In the Council's Pastoral Constitution on the Church in the Modern World, *Gaudium et spes,* the magisterium focused in a new way on the human person. For centuries, in her moral teaching the Catholic Church had emphasized natural law, that is the moral order inscribed in creation, that reflects the mind and purpose of the Creator. In the teaching of Vatican II, there was a shift from truth expressed in nature to truth embodied in the human person. The inherited method focused on nature and the "essence" of things; what was morally right or morally wrong was seen as determined by whether it was in accordance with or against nature. But this approach did not do justice to the uniqueness of the human person, who is characterized by relationships within society. In *Gaudium et spes*, the first half of the document is on "The Church and Man's Vocation" of which the first chapter is entitled "The Dignity of the Human Person".

Another important step in *Gaudium et spes* was the attempt at a greater integration of morals and faith. The older moral theology based on natural law was more philosophical than theological. Vatican II's focus on the human person made possible a moral vision that sees Jesus Christ as the perfect embodiment of the human person according to the plan of God. "Christ the Lord, Christ the new Adam, in the very revelation of the mystery of the Father and of his love, fully reveals man to himself and brings to light his most high calling" (GS, 22). This approach was to be further developed in the teaching of John Paul II and formed a key theme of his first encyclical *Redemptor hominis* (1979).

The opening of the Catholic Church to dialogue is then a facet of the Church's new consciousness of the dignity of the human person. Every human being is made in the image of God and has been created for loving communion with God and with fellow humans. The Christian vision excludes all forms of racism which deny full humanity to any group of human beings of whatever race, tribe, language or religion. Exclusion can take the form of hatred, prejudice, ridicule, or neglect. The Christian call is to love, but love must begin with dialogue. As the famous Belgian Cardinal Désiré-Joseph Mercier once said: 'We cannot love one another without knowing one another, and we cannot know one another without meeting one another.' Dialogue means meeting, it means listening and it means listening with respect.

Sources for teaching on dialogue

Paul VI, *Ecclesiam suam* (1964)

John Paul II, *Ut unum sint* (1995), para. 34

John Paul II, *Novo millennio ineunte* (2001), paras. 54 – 56

Questions for discussion

How would you define dialogue?

Why is the method of dialogue not a form of compromise?

What are the main differences between dialogue with Christians and dialogue with non-Christians?

Chapter 2

Conscience: the inner sanctuary

A key element in the dignity of the human person is the human conscience. The inner sanctuary of each person that we call the conscience is at the core of human dignity. Those who trample on human dignity do not care about the conscience. Those who seek to enhance human dignity will honour the conscience of each person. The renewal of the Church must always pass through the conscience of church members, whether in personal renewal, parish renewal, church renewal, or renewal of the world.

Our most secret core and sanctuary

"Conscience is man's most secret core, and his sanctuary. There he is alone with God whose voice echoes in his depths" (GS 16; CCC, 1795). Conscience is the place of encounter with

God. It is like the compass that God has placed within us to guide us on his paths. In the Old Testament, the longest psalm – Psalm 119 - is a wonderful meditation on God's ways and the blessedness of those who meditate on his law. This psalm is speaking of the conscience of the upright and godly person: "Your testimonies are my delight, they are my counsellors" (Ps. 119:24). "Thy word is a lamp to my feet and a light to my path." (Ps. 119:105). "I keep your precepts and testimonies, for all my ways are before you" (Ps. 119:168).

So conscience is first of all a capacity within each person to register or to receive the mind of God. It is where the law of God is inscribed on our heart. Our "dignity lies in observing this law" and by it we "will be judged" (GS, 16). This says something important about the Catholic Church's understanding of the human condition. God is not just distant and remote, until a Christian missionary arrives. All the Church documents here refer to Romans 2:14-16. What the law of Moses required for the Israelites is written on the hearts of all peoples "while their conscience also bears witness" (Rom. 2:15). The conscience is like a secret sanctuary, invisible to the world, "since what takes place in the heart of the person is hidden from the eyes of everyone outside" (VS, 57).

John Paul II speaks of "this interior dialogue of man with himself" (VS, 58), which is our inner debate how to respond to this law of God, that is not just exterior to us, but within us through God's creation. So, he says, this interior dialogue of man with himself is also "a dialogue of man with God" (VS, 58). "Conscience is the witness of God himself, whose voice and judgement penetrate the depths of man's soul, calling him ... to obedience." (VS, 58).

God's law and human freedom

An essential element in the dignity of the human person is the acceptance of responsibility. It is through conscience that we accept moral responsibility. Responsibility means the ability to respond. This word recognizes that as human beings we do not just invent our own morality, deciding for ourselves what is right and what is wrong. We are those who respond to God, the law-giver and plan-maker. Morality is learned and received; it is not invented.

In *Veritatis splendor*, Pope John Paul sets himself strongly against the widespread idea that a mature conscience means making up our own mind free from all law and authority. Christian faith believes in the Creator God, who has given us the maker's instructions in the Ten Commandments and who has revealed his overall plan for creation through his Son, Jesus, who is "the way, the truth and the life" (John 14: 6).

It is God's law, first of all in God, outside us and above us, that is "the universal and objective norm of morality" (VS, 60). But this law has to be received into our understanding and to operate through our conscience, which is "the proximate norm of personal morality" (VS, 60). God's law takes on flesh in us, as it took on flesh perfectly in Jesus. In Jesus Christ, we meet God's plan for humankind. So the Pope says: "People today need to turn to Christ once again in order to receive from him the answer to their questions about what is good and what is evil" (VS, 8).

This law of God that is within us, but originates outside us, imposes obligations: "the judgement of conscience has an imperative character: man must act in accordance with it" (VS, 60). It is only our disordered nature that experiences this demand as a burden. Jesus himself said: "My food is to do the will of him who sent me" (John 4:34). Jesus knew this was not indignity, but freedom. He delighted to do his Father's will, to "eat" this food. "I know that his [the Father's] commandment is eternal life" (John 12:50).

The formation of conscience

The human conscience is not a machine to register external commands. It is the point of exchange between the God who speaks and the creature who responds. At the beginning of our conscious lives, we do not have detailed moral knowledge; but we do know there is a right and a wrong. We know two patterns of desire: a desire to do right and to seek the ways of truth, and an urge to rebel and do what we feel like doing. The first is the deeper desire, sustained by the grace of God.

Being responsible means first seeking the truth. The famous St Augustine said to the Lord: "For you have made us for yourself and our hearts are restless till they rest in you" (Confessions). We are made to seek. We seek the truth of God. We are restless until we find that truth.

There are two sides to becoming a responsible Christian: the searching and the finding. We will not be formed unless we want to be formed. We are formed first of all by the revealed Word of God. "The Word of God is a light for our path. We must assimilate it in faith and prayer and put it into practice. This is how moral conscience is formed" (CCC, 1802). The book of Proverbs contains much wisdom on desiring formation and instruction: "Hear, my son, and accept my words, that the years of your life may be many. I have taught you the way of wisdom; I have led you in the paths of uprightness. When you walk, your step will not be hampered; and if you run, you will not stumble. Keep hold of instruction, do not let go; guard her, she is your life" (Prov. 4:10-13).

In the Catholic understanding, formation of conscience takes place as a regular element in the faith life of the Church community. It begins in the home with the responsibility of Christian parents. Catholic schools cannot do much for children by way of moral formation when a foundation has not been laid in the home. But we learn above all from how we see people behave around us. In a time when Christian moral values are no longer upheld in society, it is all the more essential that our parishes show the world what it means to live a principled and conscientious life.

As Catholics, we are blessed to be part of a Church with a living teaching authority. The encyclical *Veritatis splendor* was written to correct misleading and inadequate presentations of morality and conscience. But the basic moral formation of Christians comes first from the Word of God, and the age-long faith of the Church, expressed above all in the liturgy and preached in the homily. The teaching of the bishops and the Pope then confirms, clarifies and corrects the regular teaching in pulpit and class room, ensuring that the Church as a whole is faithful to the teaching of Christ.

The Pope corrects a common misunderstanding in his encyclical: "When the Church pronounces on moral questions, [she] in no way undermines the freedom of conscience of Christians" This is "because the Magisterium does not bring to the Christian conscience truths which are extraneous to it; rather it brings to light the truths which it ought already to possess" (VS, 64).

The power of decision

Conscience in the Catholic understanding is not just a faculty or capacity to determine right or wrong, but it is an instrument for practical decision-making. We take personal responsibility for our actions when we make the practical judgement of conscience: "this is right, and I will do it, or this is wrong, and I will not do it." One biblical narrative that brings out this practical judgement before God is the story of Joseph and Potiphar's wife. Potiphar's wife is badgering Joseph to sleep with her. Joseph is conscious of his responsibility to her husband and to God, and answers her demands: "Lo, having me my master has no concern about anything in the house, and he has put everything that he has in my hand; he is not greater in this house than I am; nor has he kept back anything from me except yourself, because you are his wife; how then can I do this great wickedness, and sin against God" (Gen. 39:8-9).

"Conscience enables one to assume responsibility for the acts performed" (CCC, 1781). We find an example in the meeting of Zacchaeus, the chief tax collector, with Jesus. It is remarkable in this story that Jesus does not seem to have preached to Zacchaeus. The tax collector had been impressed by the news of Jesus's ministry. So he climbs a tree so that he can see Jesus. Jesus decides to visit his house. Zacchaeus "made haste and came down, and received him joyfully" (Luke 19:6). Without more ado, Zacchaeus stands up and publicly tells Jesus: "Behold,

Lord, the half of my goods I give to the poor; and if I have defrauded anyone of anything, I restore it fourfold" (Luke 19:8). Tax collectors were notorious in that culture for dishonesty and for making a fortune by extortion. What had happened to Zacchaeus? He was convicted in his conscience of the wrongs he had done. But he did not keep this to himself, but announced what steps he would take to right the injustice and to make amends for his sin.

Freed from a guilty conscience

We all know the experience of a guilty conscience. When we live a life of prayer and self-examination, we know immediately when we have sinned and we feel guilty. When people have lived away from God and from prayer, their conscience needs to be awakened, like that of Zacchaeus. This shows us that it is normal and healthy to feel guilty when we sin. What is not normal is to do evil and not to feel any qualms. What is not healthy is to feel guilty but to do nothing about it.

We should welcome the pangs of conscience, and then act on them. That means confessing our sins with faith in Jesus Christ, who came into this world to save us from our sin, to be the Lamb of God who takes away the sins of the world. "If we confess our sins, he is faithful and just, and will forgive our sins and cleanse us from all unrighteousness" (1 John 1:9). We need both to confess our sin to God without delay, and seek an appropriate time to take part in the Church's mercy ministry, the sacrament of reconciliation.

The sacrament of reconciliation

It is important that we make a good examination of conscience before confession. Then we truly take responsibility for our past behaviour. The *Catechism of the Catholic Church* makes this recommendation: "The reception of this sacrament ought to be prepared for by an examination of conscience made in the light of the Word of God. The passages best suited to this can be found in the Ten Commandments, in the moral catechesis of the Gospels and the apostolic Letters, such as the Sermon on the Mount and the apostolic teachings" (CCC, 1454).

When we receive God's forgiveness in the sacrament of reconciliation, we need to believe that we are truly forgiven by the Lord. Then there will be no remaining guilt. A good examination of conscience leads through the sacrament to a purification of conscience that brings greater light for future situations and decisions.

Sources for teaching on conscience

Vatican II, *Gaudium et spes*, para. 16

Catechism of the Catholic Church, paras. 1776 – 1802

John Paul II *Veritatis splendor* (1993), paras. 54 – 64

John Paul II *Evangelium vitae* (1995), para. 24

Questions for discussion

How does Catholic teaching explain the relationship between God's law and personal conscience?

Describe your own experience of moral formation – in family, in school, in parish, in other settings.

What point struck you most from the *Catechism* or the Pope's teaching on conscience?

The Church as model community

The themes of dialogue and of conscience show how human dignity is exercised in all spheres of personal and social life. Before we start to consider particular areas of life in relation to human dignity, we will look for a moment at the role of the Church. The role of the Church as teacher runs throughout this book, which aims to summarize the teaching of the Catholic Church on the dignity of the human person. But there is another very important role of the Church that needs to be borne in mind as we look at each area of application. It is the role of the Church as model community, the example for the world of how life is lived differently when one believes in Jesus Christ, the Holy Spirit and the fatherhood of God.

In the documents of Vatican II, the Church is described as "sacrament". Here the bishops take the word "sacrament" that we Catholics have applied for centuries to the seven basic grace-conferring rites celebrated by the Church, and they apply it to the Church herself: "Rising from the dead he [Christ] sent his life-giving Spirit upon his disciples and through him set up his Body which is the Church as the universal sacrament of salvation" (LG, 48).

What does it mean to call the Church sacrament or universal sacrament? We can take some of the ideas we associate with the seven sacraments and apply them to the Church. First, the Church is a sign. But whereas we think of the seven sacraments as signs to the participants, the Church is a sign to the world. It is a sign to the world of God's plan of salvation. It is a sign to the world of the coming kingdom of God; so it points to how human society should live and operate. Secondly, the Church is an effective sign. Through the Holy Spirit making Christ present in the Church, she is a sign that transforms – not just transforming individuals, but transforming our relationships and our communities. This truth is expressed in the *Catechism:* "The Church in this world is the sacrament of salvation, the sign and instrument of the communion of God and men" (CCC, 780).

In this way, the Second Vatican Council laid the foundation for a view of the Church as "model community". This is inherently a servant role, because the Church as model community patterns herself on Jesus, who "came not to be served, but to serve"

(Matt. 20:28). As a servant community the Church brings and proclaims God's salvation to the world.

In England and Wales, this vision of the Church as model community has been presented by Cardinal Cormac Murphy-O'Connor in relation to the issue of child abuse. Presenting the hierarchy's response to this problem, the Cardinal said that the way child abuse is handled in the Catholic Church has to become a model for how society should respond. The Church's response must be based on God's revelation concerning the human person, the family and human community. In the context of child protection, it gives priority to the victims of abuse, to protection of the vulnerable, and to honouring the position of parents.

Human person in living community

The Christian vision of the human person is based on two principles that must always be held together: first, the uniqueness of each human person; second, the need to live in society. Both aspects are found in the creation account in Genesis 2. The uniqueness of each person is shown by God breathing life into the man he has created: "The Lord God ... breathed into his nostrils the breath of life; and man became a living being" (Gen. 2:7). The uniqueness of each person is rooted in the teaching "that every spiritual soul is created immediately by God – it is not 'produced' by the parents" (CCC, 366). The need to live in society is shown in the creation of the woman and then in the formation of new human life coming from the union of man and woman: "Then the Lord God said, 'It is not good that the man should be alone; I will make him a helper fit for him" (Gen. 2:18). So the Church teaches: "The human person needs to live in society. Society is not for him an extraneous addition but a requirement of his nature" (CCC, 1879).

When we emphasize the uniqueness of each person, but forget the human need to live in society, we produce an irresponsible individualism that is incapable of generating a common vision. But when we emphasize the human need for society, but overlook the unique dignity of each human being, then we produce totalitarian societies that trample on the rights and dignity of individuals in the name of social progress.

Modelling Christian community

The Catholic Church teaches the duty of each citizen to play a responsible role in society. The *Catechism* highlights the word participation. I summarize here some points from CCC, 1913 – 1917. All people participate in society according to their position and role so as to promote the common good of all. Participation means taking personal responsibility, first in the family, then at work, then in other areas including public life. Participation for the sake of the common good requires a continuing conversion in all involved.

But Church exhortations to be socially responsible will have no effect unless our church communities are forming Christians for their roles in society. In his letter *Novo millennio ineunte* (2001) John Paul II called for all Christian communities to become "schools of prayer" (NMI, 33). In a similar way, we can propose a parallel idea: our parishes as schools of formation in human responsibility and social participation.

The New Testament presents the Church as the Body of Christ. This image compares the Church community to the human body, in which there are many limbs and organs that all work together for the wellbeing of the whole. "For just as the body is one and has many members, and all the members of the body, though many, are one body, so it is with Christ" (1 Cor. 12:12). So each member of the Church is given particular gifts, "the manifestation of the Spirit for the common good" (1 Cor. 12:7). Nobody can say to anyone else that they are not needed. "The eye cannot say to the hand, 'I have no need of you,' nor again the head to the feet, 'I have no need of you.'" (1 Cor. 12:21). So the entire body of the Church works in harmony for the upbuilding of the whole: "the whole body [is] joined and knit together by every joint with which it is supplied, when each part is working properly, makes bodily growth and upbuilds itself in love." (Eph. 4:16).

It is within the local church that we are to learn the full dignity of each person as a son or daughter of the Father, and as a needed and irreplaceable member of the community. We only learn the true dignity and place of each person as we see them in relationship to God as well as in relationship to other people. This is the role of the Church as sacrament. The Church teaches us how to live in society not just by issuing documents but by modelling in the local community the lifestyle of the coming kingdom.

The role of the liturgy

When is the Church most clearly made visible? The Church's answer is – during the liturgy. And most of all in the celebration of the Eucharist. In fact, Vatican II said: "The principal manifestation of the Church consists in the full, active participation of all God's holy people in the same liturgical celebrations, especially in the same Eucharist, in one prayer, at one altar, at which the bishop presides, surrounded by his college of priests and by his ministers" (SC, 41).

We can only expect to have responsible active members of society coming from a Church that promotes responsible active participation in its own life and worship. We can ask in our parishes: how can the parish liturgy promote a sense of the dignity of each participant as a child of God? How can we encourage active participation by all present? How can we encourage the use of varied gifts and ministries within the liturgy of the Church?

A sense of service to one another within the parish will overflow into a sense of service to the needy, the handicapped and the oppressed in our society. The Church community is to model in action Christ's words about "the least of these my brethren" (Matt. 25:40): the hungry, the thirsty, the stranger, the homeless, the sick and the imprisoned. 'May we all hear those welcoming words of the king: "Come, O blessed of my Father, inherit the kingdom prepared for you from the foundation of the world"' (Matt. 25:34).

Sources for teaching on the Church as model community

Vatican II, *Lumen gentium,* para. 48

Vatican II, *Gaudium et spes,* para. 40

Questions for discussion

Do you find the description of the Church as sacrament helpful for understanding the role of the Church in the world?

Suggest practical ways in which our parishes can model ways of enhancing the dignity of the human person.

The Gospel of Life

As we consider how Church teaching on the dignity of the human person applies to various areas of human behaviour, it is appropriate to begin with the Gospel of life. For life is the first gift that each of us receives. Jesus identified his mission with life. He came that we might have life: the life of the indwelling Spirit now, and the life of the resurrection in the age to come. "I came that they may have life, and have it abundantly" (John 10: 10).

In this chapter, we will look at Pope John Paul II's encyclical letter *Evangelium vitae* [the Gospel of life], issued in 1995. A major achievement of John Paul II is the way he has reshaped the moral and social teaching of the Catholic Church. He has in a new way grounded this teaching in the Scriptures and in the great

Christian doctrines of the Incarnation, the Redemption and the Trinity. We can see this in *Evangelium vitae*. In the past, a papal letter on this subject might have been called "The Gift of Life", a good and accurate title. But this encyclical is called "The Gospel of Life". Gospel means good news. It is the word used in the Scriptures for the message of Jesus, and in particular for his resurrection from the dead. The Pope sees all the current issues about life (abortion, euthanasia, experimentation on embryos) in the total context of God's plan of creation and redemption leading to the glory of eternal life. "The Gospel of God's love for man, the Gospel of the dignity of the person and the Gospel of life are a single and indivisible Gospel" (EV, 2).

Uniquely in this encyclical, the Pope begins each section with a verse of scripture. In this way, his letter invites us to meditate on the wonder of creation: the creation of all forms of life, and particularly of human life, that is formed in the image and likeness of God. For a genuine celebration of the Gospel of life, we need "a contemplative outlook": "Such an outlook arises from faith in the God of life, who has created every individual as a 'wonder' (Ps. 139:14)" (EV, 83).

The story of Cain

Evangelium vitae begins with a rich reflection on the story of Cain and the murder of his brother Abel, found in Genesis 4:8-16. Cain is jealous of Abel. He was angry "and his countenance fell"

(Gen. 4:5). God warns Cain: "Sin is crouching at the door; its desire is for you, but you must master it" (Gen. 4:7). "Cain remains free in the face of sin" (EV, 8). But Cain sins, and kills his brother. So the apostle John says, "Be not like Cain who was of the evil one and murdered his brother" (1 John 3:12). "Man's revolt against God in the earthly paradise is followed by the deadly combat of man against man" (EV, 8).

When Cain is challenged by the Lord: "Where is Abel your brother?" (Gen. 4:9), he "tries to cover up his crime with a lie" (EV, 8). Here we find a brilliant description of how rebellion against God's law is followed by a refusal of responsibility. We see how the taking of life distorts the human conscience, and leads to excuses and rationalization. "Am I my brother's keeper?" (Gen. 4:9). "Yes, every man is his "brother's keeper", because God entrusts us to one another" (EV, 19).

God cannot leave the crime unpunished: the ground that was to be the source of blessing has now been defiled by the shedding of blood. "And now you are cursed from the ground, which has opened its mouth to receive your brother's blood from your hand" (Gen. 4:11). Cain is sent into exile, and becomes "a fugitive and a wanderer on the earth" (Gen. 4:14). But Cain is not totally rejected. In Cain's enforced exile, God places a mark upon him, not to humiliate him but to protect him "lest any who came upon him should kill him" (Gen. 4:15). "Not even a murderer loses his personal dignity, and God himself pledges to guarantee this" (EV, 9).

But it is not only the blood of Abel, the first innocent man to be murdered, which cries out to God from the ground. "The blood of every other human being who has been killed since Abel is also a voice raised to the Lord" (EV, 25). This leads the Pope to reflect on the precious blood of Jesus, "the sprinkled blood that speaks more graciously than the blood of Abel" (Heb.12:24). "The blood of Christ, while it reveals the grandeur of the Father's love, shows how precious man is in God's eyes and how priceless the value of his life" (EV, 25).

Fighting the culture of death

In our day we find ourselves in the midst of "an enormous and dramatic clash between good and evil, death and life" (EV, 28). "The twentieth century will have been an era of massive attacks on life, an endless series of wars and a continual taking of innocent human life" (EV, 17). The Pope calls this the battle between "the culture of death" and the "culture of life". The culture of death follows the way of Cain. John Paul II notes the ways in which human life is being belittled, trampled upon and extinguished: in wars and the arms trade, in degradation of the environment, in sexual exploitation, in the criminal spread of drugs (see EV, 10).

The Pope's warnings about the "culture of death" show the inter-connectedness of sins against life. The culture of death exalts the self against the plan and design of God. It exalts having over being. It regards pleasure and convenience as a right, and sees no value in suffering. "Everything is negotiable, everything is open to bargaining: even the first of the fundamental rights, the right to life" (EV, 20). But the Pope's attention is focused on the evils of abortion, of medical experimentation with human embryos and of euthanasia (EV, Section III, 58-65). Abortion is such a grave offence against life, because "the one eliminated is a human being at the very beginning of life. No one more absolutely innocent could be imagined" (EV, 58). The Pope goes on to condemn all experimentation on human embryos that does not respect the life and integrity of the human embryo. The human embryo is not just "biological material" for use as scientists and doctors may desire.

John Paul II sees voluntary euthanasia, that is "mercy killing" or "assisted suicide" as "one of the more alarming symptoms of the culture of death" (EV, 64). This trend is found above all in "prosperous societies, marked by an attitude of excessive preoccupation with efficiency" (EV, 64). So when people are no longer "useful" or "productive" then because of this efficiency mentality, they have no more value. While in extreme cases, euthanasia may seem to represent a caring attitude towards those who are suffering acutely, in fact it may represent an unwillingness to "go the extra mile".

In society today, there is a crisis in the moral sense, leading to euphemisms that call evil actions by less unpleasant names. But the Pope says: "We need now more than ever to have the courage to look the truth in the eye and to call things by their proper name" (EV, 58).

The culture of death produces an industry of death: so abortion is not just an individual evil, but gives rise to an industry, with all its vested interests and commercial promotion. So the Pope speaks of "The network of complicity which reaches out to institutions, foundations and associations which systematically campaign for the legalization and spread of abortion in the world" (EV, 59).

Evangelium vitae points out repeatedly how the disregard for life hits hardest the weak, the poor and the defenceless. The culture of death exalts the strong over the weak: the healthy over the handicapped; people in their prime over the elderly; the wealthy and the powerful over the "have nots" and the powerless. "The first to be harmed are women, children, the sick or suffering, and the elderly" (EV, 23).

Promoting the culture of life

We must not be discouraged by the apparent power of the culture of death. Our Christian confidence in the face of the culture of death comes from the victory of Jesus. We, who celebrate Easter can proclaim the joyful shout of Paul: "Death is swallowed up in victory" (1 Cor. 15:54).

To speak of the culture of life shows the inter-connectedness of all forms of life. The culture of life exists where people respect life, where people protect life, where people love life, and where people serve life (see EV, 5). We see the culture of life lived out in Christian families, in ministries like the Missionaries of Charity throughout the world and the Sisters of Life in Glasgow, in homes for the elderly, and especially in hospices for the dying, where life is treasured and reverenced as the gift of God. Each is a true witness to the Gospel of life.

However, for the Christian there is a great paradox, the paradox of the Cross: eternal life comes through a death, the sacrificial death of Jesus. "From the Cross, the source of life, the 'people of life' is born ... Life finds its centre, its meaning and its fulfilment when it is given up" (EV, 51). It is the loving obedience of Jesus unto death "even death on a cross" (Phil. 2:8) that most clearly shows forth the infinite value of every human life. In his death, we see our value. In his resurrection, we see our destiny.

To promote the culture of life, we have to die to self. As disciples of Jesus, we take up our cross to follow him. Our food is the will of the Father, expressed in the Word of God, and the bread of life, that is the body of Christ "given up for you". In the Eucharist, we feed on the One who gave his life for us, the Lamb of God, who takes away the sins of the world. In the strength of this food, we can love one another as Christ loved us (John 13: 34), we can bear one another's burdens (Gal. 6: 2), we can live lives of service. We can be servants of life.

Sources for teaching on human life

John Paul II, *Evangelium vitae*

Catechism of the Catholic Church, paras. 2258 – 2283

Questions for discussion

What does the Pope mean by "the culture of death?"

Why do you think that this might be an important phrase?

What is the link between protection of the unborn and protection of the poor and the weak in society?

Discuss how a Catholic parish can work to promote a culture of life.

Chapter 5

The dignity of the human body

In a book on the dignity of the human person, it is very important to present the Church's teaching on human sexuality. The reason for teaching on sexuality is not the same as the reason why the tabloids love stories about sex. It is because sexuality is intrinsic to the way God created the human person. God did not simply create a generic human being, God made men and women. "So God created man in his own image, in the image of God he created him; male and female he created them" (Gen. 1:27). The dignity of the human person means the dignity of men and women, the dignity of sexually differentiated beings.

The human body

We can only understand the place of human sexuality in God's plan when we have a right understanding of the dignity of the human body. Pope John Paul II has been deeply aware how critical this understanding is for the future of the Church and for the future of society. For the first six years of his pontificate, the Pope taught systematically on this subject in his weekly audiences in Rome. This teaching is gathered together in his book *The Theology of the Body: Human Love in the Divine Plan* (TB).

In the Church's understanding, the human body is part of being human. "Man, though made of body and soul, is a unity" (GS, 14). The human body is the means and the form of human self-expression. Through our bodies we express our inner thoughts and our inner desires. Through our bodies we relate to each other, and through our bodies we communicate with others in words, in gestures and in facial expressions.

Through our bodies too, we form human society and culture. When Thomas Merton wrote *No Man is an Island*, he knew that as bodily beings we are dependent upon one another. We are born into a family. As babies and children, we are vulnerable and dependent creatures needing the love and care of our parents for survival and growth. The family into which we are born belongs to a tribe, people or nation. We have relatives, we belong to a neighbourhood, we go to school. To be truly human is to belong.

So it is no accident that our languages use the word "body" not only for the physical body, but also for corporate entities, like bodies of people.

So when God sends his Son to redeem the human race, he is "born of a woman" (Gal. 4: 4), and becoming man he takes on a human body. "Consequently, when Christ came into the world, he said: 'Sacrifices and offerings thou hast not desired, but a body hast thou prepared for me" (Heb. 10: 5). So when Jesus offers his life for us, he does so in and through his body. When he says at the Last Supper, "This is my body", he is not saying, "This is a part of me". He is saying "this is me; this is my whole life, given up for you through my body." The apostle Paul had a great insight into the gift of the body. He knew that eucharistic communion is a sharing in the body of Christ. "The bread which we break, is it not a participation in the body of Christ?" (1 Cor. 10: 16). But he saw that as we Christians feed on the same body of Christ, we are formed into one body. "Because there is one bread, we who are many are one body, for we all partake of the one bread" (1 Cor. 10:17).

The dignity of the human body is shown forth in the incarnation of the Son of God. The body of Jesus is the dwelling place of the Most High. This in turn tells us of the dignity of human fellowship as it is purified and elevated in the Church that is the body of Christ. The way we view the human body speaks volumes about our view of life.

In our day, there has been a devaluation and degradation of the human body. Often the body is just seen as a "possession", like any other material object we own. So people can even say "I have a right to do what I want with my body." But my body is myself. I do not have a right to do whatever I feel like doing, irrespective of right or wrong, irrespective of all consequences. A materialistic view of the human body produces a lack of respect for human life. In *Evangelium vitae* the Pope says: "The body is no longer perceived as a proper personal reality, a sign and place of relations with others, with God and with the world. It is reduced to pure materiality: it is simply a complex of organs, functions and energies to be used according to the sole criteria of pleasure and efficiency" (EV, 23).

Through our redemption in Christ, the Holy Spirit comes to dwell within us. St Paul tells the Corinthians: "Do you not know that your body is a temple of the Holy Spirit within you, which you have from God? You are not your own; you were bought with a price. So glorify God in your body" (1 Cor. 6:19-20). So the Pope affirms "the inseparable connection between the person, his life and his bodiliness" (EV, 81). This is why the Church has always preferred burial to cremation: though today the Church permits cremation "provided that it does not demonstrate a denial of faith in the resurrection of the body" (CCC, 2301).

Man and woman

In the second creation story in the book of Genesis, the man knows that he is different from the animals and other living beings. He names them all "but for the man there was not found a helper fit for him" (Gen. 2:20). In this way, the biblical author introduces the theme of relationship: human beings are made for relationship and fellowship. "God created man and woman together and willed each for the other" (CCC, 371).

When the man first sees the woman, he utters a cry of recognition and joy: "This at last is bone of my bones and flesh of my flesh" (Gen. 2:23). Here there is a recognition of equality of dignity and of difference in mutuality. "The woman is another 'I' in a common humanity. From the very beginning they appear as a 'unity of the two': and this signifies that the original solitude is overcome" (MD, 6). Man and woman are first alone, but are then brought together in a "communion of persons" (TB, 46). This is still our experience: we have first to experience our human aloneness, before entering into mature relationships.

Man and woman are complementary. Our world cannot exist without women and men. Both have distinctive gifts and characteristics. "In their 'being man' and 'being woman,' they reflect the Creator's wisdom and goodness." (CCC, 369). The differences between women and men are profound, and not just genital. Any kind of "unisex" ideology is unacceptable to Christians, because it dehumanizes what it means to be woman or man, reducing gender to the merely physical. The biblical understanding of the body is always that the physical expresses and embodies the spiritual. The woman's bodily make-up manifests her orientation to receptivity, to conception, to nurture and relationship, while the man's constitution has greater physical strength for his tasks in the world around him. Today we have to be careful not to use the differences between man and woman to justify forms of masculine domination and feminine marginalization without falling into an ideological uniformity that ignores the particular giftings and qualities of each gender. Our protection here is an insistence on the equal dignity of women and men, both created in the image and likeness of God and both called to the same eternal destiny.

Sexual relationship

The male – female relationship finds its distinctive expression in marriage. So the biblical narrative continues: "Therefore a man leaves his father and his mother and cleaves to his wife, and they become one flesh" (Gen. 2:24). Jesus cites this verse in his rejection of divorce: "So they are no longer two but one flesh. What therefore God has joined together, let no man put asunder" (Matt. 19:6). Here we can see the roots of the Church's firm conviction that sexual relationship belongs to the nature of marriage as a lifelong union.

The meaning of sex in marriage flows from the biblical

understanding of the body as visible expression of the acting person. The coming together of man and woman in sexual union expresses in bodily form the deepest giving of one person to another that is humanly possible. The Pope says that "the human body speaks a 'language' which it is not the author of ... the most profound words of the spirit – words of love, of giving, of fidelity – demand an adequate language of the body" (TB, 359). That language is marital sex. That is why casual sex dehumanizes and trivializes the deepest things in God's creation.

The nature of sex as God has created it expresses lifelong commitment. Each act of marital union expresses the desire for total self-giving, which to be authentic must be "for keeps". "Love seeks to be definitive; it cannot be an arrangement 'until further notice' " (CCC, 1646). Each act in love forms and deepens the couple in their marriage. This is the meaning of the Church's teaching that Christian marriage is a sacrament. Each act of marital self-giving expresses the fullness of the final union of Christ and the Church, and contributes towards its realization.

Our need for salvation

The Pope's teaching on human sexuality emphasizes that all human beings need redemption, for our sexuality has been affected by the rebellion of sin. The original goodness of sexuality has not been destroyed, but it has been damaged by human self-will and selfishness. The Christian call to holy sex in marriage involves a call to purification from all lust that degrades the other. "For this is the will of God, your sanctification: that you abstain from unchastity; that each one of you know how to take a wife for himself in holiness and honour not in the passion of lust like heathens who do not know God … For God has not called us for uncleanness, but in holiness" (1 Thess. 4:3-5, 7).

Lust is "the relationship of possession of the other as the object of one's own desire" (TB, 123), the opposite of self-giving in love. So the Pope in his teachings on human sexuality keeps returning to the theme of "the redemption of the body". He explains that in the New Testament, the victory over sin has been decisively won in the resurrection of Jesus, but that the hope for the deliverance of the body is eschatological, awaiting the resurrection of the dead on the last day. But precisely in this time of the Church between the first and the second comings of the Lord, the grace of Christ is given for the overcoming of the sin tendencies that remain within us. St Paul teaches not only, "Let not sin reign in your mortal bodies, to make you obey their passions" (Rom. 6:12), but also, "If by the Spirit you put to death the deeds of the body you will live" (Rom. 8:13).

The Pope sees a particular significance in Paul's teaching in Ephesians 5 on Christ's self-giving as bridegroom to his bride, the Church. "That gift of himself to the Father by obedience unto death (cf. Phil. 2:8) is contemporaneously, according to Ephesians, a 'giving himself up for the Church.' In this expression, redeeming love is transformed, I would say, into spousal love." (TB, 314). In the marital relationship, which is sacramental, the grace of Christ transforms the believing couple from within. This love of the Christian couple is fed in each Eucharist, in which the divine bridegroom gives himself afresh to his bride. In the gift of the body of Christ, Christians receive the Lamb once offered, as they "proclaim the Lord's death until he comes" (1 Cor.11: 26).

Sources for teaching on the human body and sexuality

John Paul II *The Theology of the Body: Human Love in the Divine Plan* (Pauline Books and Media)

John Paul II *Evangelium vitae,* paras. 23, 81

Catechism of the Catholic Church, paras. 369 -373

Questions for discussion

How do we know that our bodies are not just external instruments but fully part of our human identity?

What does the Pope mean by the "language of the body" in marriage?

Discuss how marriage as a sacrament contributes to the inner sanctification of our deepest desires.

Chapter 6

The dignity of the family

Throughout his ministry as Pope, John Paul II has emphasized that the family is "the way of the Church". The Church's teaching on the family represents an age-long teaching being revivified and deepened through the biblical and ecclesial renewal of Vatican II. At the heart of this renewed understanding are: (1) the dignity of the human person created in the image of God for personal communion with God and with other persons; and (2) the church as the communion or family of the redeemed, united with Jesus Christ in the power of the Holy Spirit to the glory of the Father.

The family, a communion of persons

What do we associate with family? Family means home. Home means safety, a place of warmth and welcome. Children cry and play, are loved and trained. Family also means uncles, aunts and cousins. The Pope calls this rich human reality of family "a community of persons: of husband and wife, of parents and children, of relatives" (LF, 18).

In God's plan, the family is the setting where new life comes into being and is nourished, formed and developed. In other words, in the family we discover what it means to be persons: having our own identity, with father and mother, part of a bigger family of clan, tribe and nation; being able to speak and to hear, to laugh and to cry, to be loved and to love. Here we first learn that we have rights and responsibilities, where we live under authority so as to learn how to exercise authority. So we also rebel, and learn to repent; we learn to ask for forgiveness and to receive it.

Of course the reality is not always like this. Many families are dysfunctional, often because the parents never experienced authentic family and real love in their own childhood. But God provides. We are not condemned to a vicious circle of ever-greater deterioration from generation to generation. God sends his Son to identify with human sin and failure, and to make us a new creation. But God also gives us a plan and a vision, an ideal that is not impossible because it is given by God, and because

God has sent us his Son and his Spirit. So the first of the commandments after those concerning God is about our parents: "Honour your father and your mother, that your days may be long in the land which the Lord your God gives you" (Ex. 20:12). Right from the beginning of Israel's history, God teaches his people the direct connection between honour in the family, long life and a healthy society.

The Catholic Church has long insisted that "the family is the original cell of social life" (CCC, 2207). The family existed before any nation or state came into being, and so no state has the right to interfere with family life. The priority of the family is expressed very biblically in the blessing of the wedding liturgy: "Father, by your plan man and woman are united and married life has been established as the one blessing that was not forfeited by original sin or washed away in the flood".

What is new here is the emphasis on the personal and the idea of communion. This development owes much to the life and thought of John Paul II, who, even before he was elected Pope, saw the devastating effects of Nazi and Communist dictatorship on human life and dignity. He saw the break-up and the suffering of families. He saw the need for the Church to have a more adequate philosophy of the human person. At the heart of the human is the capacity to love: "Without love the family is not a community of persons and ... without love the family cannot live, grow and perfect itself as a community of persons" (FC, 18).

This calling to love applies at all stages of family life from when a couple are first married to when the children have all left home. "All members of the family, each according to his or her own gift, have the grace and responsibility of building, day by day, the communion of persons, making the family 'a school of deeper humanity': this happens where there is care and love for the little ones, the sick, the aged; where there is mutual service every day; when there is a sharing of goods, of joys and of sorrows" (FC, 21). God leads each couple through a school of formation over many years. The demands of courtship, of the first year of marriage, of pregnancy and babies, of schooling and then of adolescence: these all make a huge range of demands on each couple. All are a challenge to grow in love: the spouses for each other, the parents for each child.

The responsibility of families to care for the elderly is not always well understood. The biblical tradition emphasized the honouring of the old and the contribution they have to make: "What an attractive thing is judgment in grey-haired men, and for the aged to possess good counsel!" (Sir. 25: 4). People today can sometimes think that all the elderly need is food, medical care and a television set. But the deepest human need is for relationships. The denial of this "causes acute suffering to [the elderly] and spiritually impoverishes many families" (FC, 27).

The Pope uses the word "communion" to open up the deeper meaning of love. Married love is inter-personal sharing, a deep and lasting meeting of minds and hearts, a sharing of all one is, expressed and symbolized in the two becoming one flesh. Without the family, the world would starve for love. This is the great calling of the family: it "has the mission to guard, reveal and communicate love" (FC, 17).

The Christian family within the Church

Just as the Church is called to be a sign of what human society should be, so the Christian family should be a sign of what all families are called to be. As each family is a basic cell of society, so each Christian family is a basic cell of the Church. This fundamental relationship between the family and the Church led to Vatican II calling the Christian family a "domestic church".

In the Christian family, all share in the gift of the Holy Spirit poured out by the risen Lord on the Church. Here the call to love is explicitly the call to love as Jesus loved: "A new commandment I give to you, that you love one another; even as I have loved you, that you also love one another" (John 13:34).

As a domestic church, the Christian family is a small community of the redeemed, mirroring the shared life of grace to the Church and the world. "Christian married couples and parents ... not only receive the love of Christ and become a saved community, but they are also called upon to communicate Christ's love to their brethren, thus becoming a saving community" (FC, 49). "Within a family that is aware of this gift, as Paul VI wrote, 'all the members evangelize and are evangelized' (FC, 39).

Calling the Christian family a domestic church points to the place of worship in the Christian home, along with the role of the Word of God. The parents as children of God honour and recognize the place of God in their lives and in their family by praying and worshipping together in the home: "by praying with their children, by reading the Word of God with them and by introducing them deeply through Christian initiation into the Body of Christ ... they become fully parents, ... begetters not only of bodily life but also of the life that ... flows from the Cross and Resurrection of Christ" (LF, 39).

As is expressed clearly in the rite of baptism for infants, "By virtue of their ministry of educating, parents are, through the witness of their lives, the first heralds of the Gospel for their children" (LF, 39). Children first learn forgiveness and reconciliation at home. For family members are not just loving and beautiful; they are also sinners, who rebel and who hurt and destroy. If children do not learn basic Christian attitudes from their parents, the later teaching in school and parish is not likely to have much impact.

Many families include members who are handicapped: children who are blind or deaf, children with Down's syndrome, children in wheelchairs. Here, too, Christian families reflect the human condition, but show forth the compassion of Jesus, as the handicapped are loved and accepted as fully part of the family. "Truly, I say to you, as you did it to one of the least of these my brethren, you did it to me" (Matt. 25:40). As the work of Jean Vanier and his community of *L'Arche* have shown, the handicapped are not just objects of charity, but sources of great blessing to those around them.

The renewal of family life

In his post-synodal letter on the vocation and mission of the laity in the Church, the Holy Father said: "The daily life itself of a truly Christian family makes up the first 'experience of Church'" (CL, 62). In this light, we can see the importance of the renewal of family life for the renewal of the Church. At the same time as family life has come under new pressures in our society, we find new movements within the Church for the renewal of family life. One of the first was the *Teams of Our Lady*, founded in France just before World War II. Well-known too is *Worldwide Marriage Encounter*, founded in the USA in the 1960s. More recently, the *Chemin Neuf* community from France has seen major fruit from its *Cana* course for the evangelization and renewal of family life.

With the Holy Father, we can sum up the calling of the Christian family: "The family should become a preparation for the communion of saints" (LF, 14).

Sources for teaching on the family

John Paul II *Familiaris consortio* (1981)

John Paul II *Christifideles laici* (1988), paras 40, 62

John Paul II *Letter to families* (1994)

Catechism of the Catholic Church, paras. 2201 - 2233

Questions for discussion

How can the idea of "communion" deepen our understanding of family life?

What does it mean for the Christian family to be called a domestic church?

Share experiences of any participation in groups aiming at the renewal of family life.

Chapter 7

Leisure with dignity

Holidays form an important part of our lives, both in anticipation and in reality. Who does not spend time in the winter and the spring dreaming of summer holidays in hot and exotic places? We all know that the travel agencies produce their summer holiday brochures ready for the Christmas and New Year break. Such breaks are also a good occasion to reflect on the place of leisure in our lives, and to see leisure in the context of the dignity of the human person.

More leisure

In most countries where English is the first language, people now have much more leisure than their ancestors ever enjoyed. For those who have work there are longer holidays; in Europe today it is normal for employees to have four weeks of paid holiday. There is also a move towards a shorter working week. Many work part-time, which may also mean more leisure time, whether enforced or chosen. Many young people take a year or two touring the world before deciding what to do with their lives. For an older generation, there is often earlier retirement, perhaps following on compulsory redundancy. People are also living longer. As a result many people begin a new life after they have officially retired. This is often the case with committed Christians, who find new scope for Christian service in their retirement years.

A privilege of the well-to-do

However, when we speak of increased leisure, we are really only speaking of a minority of the world's population. In many nations, only the wealthy elite enjoy much leisure. For the people who have inadequate incomes, insufficient food and minimal health care, leisure does not exist. Their focus is survival: how to find food, how to find treatment for disease, how to have a roof over their heads. Even in the more affluent societies of the West, there is an "underclass" of poor and homeless, for whom leisure has little meaning.

A Christian reflection on leisure faces us with this drastic contrast between the rich and the poor, between the "haves" and the "have nots". The Pope has recently written: "Our world is entering the new millennium burdened by the contradictions of an economic, cultural and technological progress which offers immense possibilities to a fortunate few, while leaving millions of others not only on the margins of progress but in living conditions far below the minimum demanded by human dignity" (NMI, 50). As we Christians who belong to "the fortunate few" reflect on human leisure, we are challenged to develop lifestyles that share the wealth of the world in place of those that merely aim to protect all we have from the less fortunate.

Celebration of the Lord's day

There is not much explicit teaching on leisure in the official teaching of the Catholic Church. Most references come in the context of teaching on the meaning of Sunday, the "Lord's day". The *Catechism* says here that: "If God 'rested and was refreshed' on the seventh day, man too ought to 'rest' and should let others, especially the poor, be 'refreshed' " (CCC, 2172). More recently still in 1998, Pope John Paul II issued a detailed letter on the Lord's Day (*Dies domini*). The right of all human beings to "enjoy the freedom, rest and relaxation which human dignity requires" (DD, 66) is dependent on God, the author of life and the author of joy. In the Pope's teaching, "the day of God" is the "day of man" because it is first the day of the Lord, the day of worship. We are created to worship. It is as we worship and recognize God's place that we will have the capacity to order human relationships and society aright.

In this context, the Pope speaks of the need to celebrate. "We humans need to rejoice. The apostle Paul told the Christians of Philippi, "Rejoice in the Lord always; and again I will say, Rejoice" (Phil. 4: 4). The right order in God's creation is that we rejoice in God, we rejoice in Jesus, we rejoice in his resurrection, we rejoice in God's promises, and then we rejoice in each other and in all the gifts of the Lord. Joy is the fruit of the Holy Spirit, that Paul lists next after love" (Gal. 5:22). We have to come to God in Jesus Christ to receive his Spirit so as to celebrate his love and his gifts. So, the Pope says: "Sunday is the day of joy in a very special way, indeed the day most suitable for learning how to rejoice and to rediscover the true nature and deep roots of joy" (DD, 57).

The Holy Father is trying to reclaim for Christians a sense of God's special day that is different from the rest of the week. In fact, this is an area where Christians can learn from the Jews, who have in many ways been more faithful in observing the Sabbath every Friday evening and Saturday than Christians have been in honouring the Day of the Resurrection. We Christians can learn much from the way that the Jewish people truly celebrate their feasts with rejoicing.

Pleasure and fun

Most of us look forward to weekends and holidays. Many live their future breaks in advance, dreaming of the fun they are going to have. Sometimes the pleasure may seem to be more in the advance anticipation than in the eventual reality. We see here a common desire for pleasure and for fun. This is what holidays and vacation breaks are for. It is all part of the human search for happiness. Pleasure and fun seem to equal happiness.

But what is the reality? People who just seek their own pleasure and fun are never truly happy. The emptiness of a life lived for fun and pleasure becomes more evident as the years go by. "He who loves pleasure will be a poor man; he who loves wine and oil will not be rich" (Prov. 21:17).

True happiness is the joy of which the Pope speaks. He says: "This joy should never be confused with shallow feelings of satisfaction and pleasure, which inebriate the senses and emotions for a brief moment, but then leave the heart unfulfilled and perhaps even embittered" (DD, 57). Joy comes from our right relationship to God. Joy comes from sharing the gifts of God. So the Christian gospel points to a deep paradox in life: when we give of ourselves, we are happy; when we grasp for ourselves, we are unhappy. This is what Jesus taught: "For whoever would save his life will lose it; and whoever loses his life for my sake, he will save it" (Luke 9:24).

A different way

Christians then have a responsibility to show the world a different way of enjoying our free time. God has created us to enjoy his gifts – first, the gift of his Son and his Spirit, and then the gift of our fellow humans. We are created to enjoy the praise of God. We are created to enjoy friendship, to learn what it is to love. We are created to recognize and appreciate beauty – in nature, in art, in developing creative skills. We need to exercise our talents, our minds and our bodies. Many will remember the movie *Chariots of Fire* telling the story of how a devout Scottish Christian, Eric Liddell, won a gold medal for his running at the Olympic Games. One memorable moment is when Liddell expresses the joy that he gets from his running and how he experiences this as the presence of God.

To enjoy God's world in a way that will bring lasting joy, we have to cast off the spirit of hedonism – of self first, of my pleasure at all costs. We have to develop a sharing spirit, a desire to appreciate rather than to possess. To do this, we have to live our lives as gift of God. This means becoming grateful believers, who thank God daily for all his blessings. As Christians, we can make sure that when we are at the beach or in the mountains, we pray daily and read the Word of God daily. For those who use a magazine like Bible Alive, maybe you can spend a little longer than usual each day on your daily reflection. Each morning or evening as a family or as a group of friends, we can thank the

Lord for the joys and pleasures of the previous day. We can ask ourselves what will give others pleasure besides me.

If we travel abroad, as so many do, we can take the opportunity to appreciate a different culture, different food, different customs, different scenery. When we go to church on Sunday, seek to appreciate how Mass is celebrated in another country – even if we do not understand the local language. Modern mobility and tourism can be a force for greater understanding in the world, but only if we are open to learn, open to appreciate, open to receive what is different. We can find out something about the country we are visiting during the months before we travel: about its history, its art, its trials and sufferings. We can plan to visit a place important in that nation's history, maybe a museum, perhaps a shrine of Our Lady or of a local saint. When we eat out at a restaurant, we can choose well loved local dishes, rather than their version of roast beef or fish and chips. Learning another language is an important way of increasing understanding. When we speak in the language of the others, even in a faltering way, we are honouring their nation and their culture. Understanding the local language will increase hugely our awareness and our enjoyment. All these are ways in which leisure enhances rather than demeans human dignity.

Sources for teaching on leisure

Catechism of the Catholic Church, paras. 2184 – 2188

John Paul II *Dies domini* (1998)

Questions for discussion

Why is there less Catholic teaching on leisure than on work?

What is the difference between joy and fun?

How can we enjoy our leisure in a more Christian way?

Chapter 8

The dignity of human work

The order of treatment has followed the pattern of our lives. The first gift is the gift of life, and we receive the gift of life as part of a family. In our families as children, we have our first experience of leisure and play. But now we need to look at another major area of human activity, that only begins as we leave childhood behind: the sphere of work. Work impacts our lives in profound ways. Most people spend a considerable portion of their lives at work. This chapter will look at how the work factor impacts on human dignity.

Pope John Paul II is one of the few Popes who has had personal experience of manual labour. During World War II under the Nazi occupation, Karol Wojtyla worked for four years in a quarry for a chemical company. This often harsh experience must have shaped his thinking on work and human dignity. Almost forty years later, work is the first specific topic he will address as Pope in an encyclical letter, known as *Laborem exercens* (1981). His stated intention is to draw out "from the heritage of the Gospel 'what is new and what is old' " (LE, 2.1). He notes how the social teaching of Leo XIII and Pius XI had focused on the rights of workers and how with Blessed John XXIII and Paul VI the focus changed to issues of wealth and poverty, and the disparity between the developed and the undeveloped world. But while drawing on the tradition of his predecessors, John Paul II brings to the theme of work his own distinctive emphasis on the dignity of the human person, rooted in the Scriptures and expressed in the person of Jesus Christ.

The worker in God's image

The biblical foundation for a "spirituality of work" is found in God's command to the first man and woman: "Be fruitful and multiply, and fill the earth and subdue it; and have dominion over the fish of the sea and over the birds of the air and over every living thing that moves upon the earth" (Gen. 1:28). So the Pope writes: "Man is the image of God partly through the mandate received from his Creator to subdue, to dominate, the earth. In carrying out this mandate, man, every human being, reflects the very action of the Creator of the universe" (LE, 4.2).

Here we can see that the Pope is writing about work in a broad sense. What he writes about work applies, not only to traditional jobs with regular salaries and wages, but also to the more varied patterns of today when many work from their own homes or may have more than one job.

A major new element in *Laborem exercens* is the teaching on work as an activity of the human person (work in the subjective sense). Work is not just considered in its objective sense of what it produces, but also as the activity of a human being, who is creative and responsible. Whether operating a conveyor belt, directing a TV programme, serving in restaurants, or working at computers, people at work are using their skills and intelligence, potentially developing a spirit of service and collaboration with others. "Through work, man not only transforms nature, adapting it to his own needs, but he also achieves fulfilment as a human being and indeed, in a sense, becomes 'more a human being' " (LE, 9.3). Later, this personalist philosophy is again applied: "Since work in its subjective aspect is always a personal action, an *actus personae*, it follows that the whole person, body and spirit, participates in it, whether it is manual or intellectual work" (LE, 24.1).

Unemployment is "in all cases an evil" (LE, 18.1), for it removes an essential element in human dignity. When it becomes widespread, "it … can become a real social disaster" (LE, 18.1). Work is "a fundamental right of all human beings" (LE, 18.3).

Those who are unemployed for long periods often lose motivation for life, and are more vulnerable to destructive forms of behaviour. "Unemployment almost always wounds its victim's dignity and threatens the equilibrium of his life" (CCC, 2436). The Pope insists on the responsibility of society, nationally and internationally, to plan and collaborate in the provision of work opportunities. This planning and organization of human labour should promote balance "between the different kinds of employment: work on the land, in industry, in the various services, white-collar work and scientific or artistic work, in accordance with the capacities of individuals and for the common good of each society and of the whole of mankind" (LE, 18.5). Major decisions concerning work which affect the welfare of whole societies, such as the opening and closing of factories, should not be made on economic grounds alone.

Work and the family

The Pope sees a strong connection between work and the family. First of all, "work is a condition for making it possible to found a family, since the family requires the means of subsistence which man normally gains through work" (LE, 10.1). In the family, children are educated to take their place in society, and are trained to do tasks in the home: "the family is simultaneously a community made possible by work and the first school of work, within the home, for every person" (LE, 10.2).

The Pope repeats the call for a "just remuneration" adequate to support family life: "either through ... a family wage – that is, a single salary given to the head of the family for his work, sufficient for the needs of the family without the other spouse having to take up gainful employment outside the home – or through other social measures such as family allowances or grants to mothers devoting themselves exclusively to their families" (LE, 19.3).

Work and society

The duty to work flows from each person's place in society. In biblical times, the book of Ecclesiasticus speaks of the contribution to social life made by each worker: the ploughman, the craftsman, the smith, the potter. "All these rely upon their hands, and each is skilful in his own work. Without them a city cannot be established, and men can neither sojourn nor live there. Yet they are not sought out for the council of the people, nor do they attain eminence in the public assembly. ... But they keep stable the fabric of the world, and their prayer is in the practice of their trade " (Sir. 38:31-34).

The Holy Father expresses the social dimension of work in this way: "Man must work out of regard for others, especially his own family, but also for the society he belongs to, the country of which he is a child, and the whole human family of which he is a member" (LE, 16.2). No one works just for himself or herself.

"More than ever, work is work with others and work for others" (CA, 32). This responsibility to contribute to society flows not only from present day relationships, but from the past and the future. This is because each person "is the heir to the work of generations and at the same time a sharer in building the future of those who will come after" (LE, 16.2).

The Pope is keenly aware of the sufferings of the exploited and of those on the margins of society. The encyclical explicitly mentions the disabled and the handicapped. "They, too, are fully human persons with gifts, rights and responsibilities: "they should be helped to participate in the life of society in all its aspects and at all the levels accessible to their capacities" (LE, 22.1). "It is a major scandal that "conspicuous natural resources remain unused, there are huge numbers of people who are unemployed or underemployed and countless multitudes of people suffering from hunger" (LE, 18.6).

The right to group together

Ever since the time of Leo XIII, the Popes have insisted on the right of all workers to form unions to defend their own interests as workers. John Paul II develops this from the fundamental human right of association, which in the work context means "defending the vital interests of those employed in the various professions." He adds that "each profession has its own specific character which should find a particular reflection" (LE, 20.1) in their unions. The Pope rejects Marxist views about the inevitability of class conflict: trade unions are primarily "for" not just "against". They are "a mouthpiece for the struggle for social justice … but it is not a struggle 'against' others" (LE, 20.3). Work, he says, "unites people". "In this consists its social power: the power to build a community" (LE, 20.3). For owners, managers and managed are all a necessary part of the human community. For this reason, "Union demands cannot be turned into a kind of group or class 'egoism'" (LE, 20.4).

The spirituality of human work

The last section of *Laborem exercens* is devoted to "the spirituality of work". Here, the Pope draws attention to the example of Jesus himself: "he belongs to the 'working world,' he has appreciation and respect for human work" (LE, 26.1). He who, "while being God, became like us in all things devoted most of the years of his life on earth to manual work at the carpenter's bench" (LE, 6.5). Because of who Jesus is, his labours were a sanctification of human work.

Here the Pope draws upon another strand concerning work from the book of Genesis. The human rebellion of the fall means that work becomes burdensome. "Cursed is the ground because of you; in toil you shall eat of it all the days of your life; thorns and thistles it shall bring forth to you" (Gen. 3: 17-18). As a result, work always to some degree involves sweat and toil. As we accept in faith this penalty for human sin, work acquires a redemptive dimension. "By enduring the toil of work in union with Christ crucified for us, man in a way collaborates with the Son of God for the redemption of humanity" (LE, 27.3).

Because issues of work and unemployment affect us not only personally but also our local communities, it is particularly important that this subject is discussed in our parishes. *Laborem exercens* can provide an excellent basis for discussion groups. Relating these issues to our faith in God and in Christ is essential if we are to live our whole lives as Christians and if we are as a Church to impact our world.

Sources for teaching on work

John Paul II, *Laborem exercens* (1981)

John Paul II, *Centesimus annus* (1991), paras. 31 – 32

Catechism of the Catholic Church, paras. 2427 – 2436

Questions for discussion

Do you find your work humanly fulfilling?

What more can be done to realize this ideal?

Does the concept of a "living wage" still mean anything in an age of "downsizing" and globalisation?

How much unemployment is there in your vicinity?

What agencies are trying to deal with this problem?

How do you see the role of the Churches?

Chapter

9

Human solidarity

Solidarity is a word that we rarely used before the late 1970s. Most likely it came to our attention first when groups of Polish workers took the bold step in a Communist nation of forming a trade union. The movement was called Solidarnosc, Polish for solidarity. We may remember television scenes from the shipyards of Danzig, a solidarity stronghold under the leadership of Lech Walesa, where the workers resisted the government attempts to shut down the trade union.

It was about this time that the word solidarity became a regular term in official Catholic teaching. This was not a coincidence. For both usages were influenced by the writing and teaching of Karol Wojtyla, who in 1978 became Pope John Paul II. The workers who formed the Solidarity trade union had been strongly influenced by the Oasis retreat movement, founded in Poland by Fr Franciszek Blacknicki, who was in close touch with the then Mgr Wojtyla. The Solidarity trade union embodied the ideals of Archbishop Wojtyla. This is one reason why the struggles between Solidarity and the Communist government never led to violent confrontation. When Archbishop, then Cardinal, Wojtyla became Pope, the concept of solidarity was an intrinsic element in his teaching on the dignity of the human person. Some years later, John Paul II reflected: "It cannot be forgotten that the fundamental crisis of systems claiming to express the rule and indeed the dictatorship of the working class began with the great upheavals which took place in Poland in the name of solidarity" (CA, 23).

What is solidarity?

Pope Paul VI had mentioned "the duty of human solidarity" in his letter *Populorum progressio.* For Paul VI, this meant "the aid that the rich nations must give to developing countries" (PP, 44, 48). On the three duties – of human solidarity, of social justice and of universal charity – "depends the future of the civilization of the world" (PP, 44).

With John Paul II, solidarity becomes a key philosophical concept. His first encyclical, *Redemptor hominis,* speaks of "the principle of solidarity". The Pope speaks of the need to transform "the structures of economic life" and says: "The task requires resolute commitment by individuals and peoples that are free and linked in solidarity" (RH, 16). We can see from this citation that for the Pope, solidarity is an essential concept for expressing the bonding of people for common action in society. Our unfamiliarity with such an idea is itself an indicator of how much we are influenced by an individualistic and often self-centred way of viewing the world.

It may be that the Pope's teaching on solidarity grew out of his reflection on the problems of human alienation in the workplace. In his encyclical letter *Laborem exercens* he has a heading, "Worker Solidarity" (LE, 8). But here, in fact, the Pope is summarizing the contributions of past Popes, especially Leo XIII, to the understanding of workers' rights, and he interprets them as urging solidarity, although they did not use this term.

An important reference to solidarity occurs in the Pope's letter *Familiaris consortio* on family life. He sees the family as "the first and irreplaceable school of social life". "It is in the family that the child learns the law of "free-giving" in the form of "heartfelt acceptance, encounter and dialogue, disinterested availability, generous service and deep solidarity" (FC, 43).

But it is in the encyclical *Sollicitudo rei socialis* that John Paul II develops his understanding of solidarity, especially in paras. 38 – 40. The Pope sees how deep are the problems in the world today. He insists that more than technical change is needed. What has to change is the human heart. The Pope hopes that all those concerned for "a more human life" for their fellow human beings "will become fully aware of the urgent need to change the spiritual attitudes which define each individual's relations with self, with neighbour, with even the remotest human communities, and with nature itself" (SRS, 38). We have to recognize our "interdependence" with others, near and far. As this interdependence becomes part of our inner attitude, it takes on the quality of a virtue, the virtue of solidarity.

The "structures of sin" that so shape our world, often based on human greed and the thirst for power, can only be overcome "by a diametrically opposed attitude: a commitment to the good of one's neighbour with the readiness, in the gospel sense, to 'lose oneself' for the sake of the other instead of exploiting him, and to 'serve him' instead of oppressing him for one's own advantage (cf. Matt. 10: 40 – 42; 20: 25; Mark 10: 42 – 45; Luke 22: 25 – 27)" (SRS, 38). The vision of an interdependent world bound together in solidarity is another way of expressing what Pope Paul VI had called a "civilization of love". But the focus on solidarity as a virtue points directly to our responsibility and our need to be transformed. A civilization of love cannot exist without virtuous citizens.

Solidarity is based upon mutual recognition as human persons (SRS, 39). Solidarity means seeing the other "whether a person, people or nation – not just as some kind of instrument, with a work capacity and physical strength to be exploited at low cost and then discarded when no longer useful, but as our 'neighbour', a 'helper' to be made a sharer, on a par with ourselves, in the banquet of life to which all are equally invited by God" (SRS, 39).

The relevance of solidarity today

In the world today it seems that many nations are becoming more fearful and self-protective. It is easy for political leaders, who have to face re-election every few years, to pay more attention to opinion polls than to the needs of poorer nations and the requirements of international justice. As the world becomes more unstable, perhaps due to flagrant injustice, people are less willing to make sacrifices for the sake of justice and the well-being of the most oppressed. Here the Pope's call for the practice of the virtue of solidarity is a cry to break out of this vicious circle of self-protection and mistrust. Either we practice solidarity or we risk world catastrophe.

It is no accident that this teaching on human solidarity as a virtue developed under communist tyranny. For it is an assertion of the inter-connectedness of all human beings, but in a Christian framework that insists on human freedom and human dignity. The communist philosophy saw the need for protection from individual greed, but its collectivist solution sacrificed human dignity and personal liberty. In the days of Soviet communism, the fear of communist revolution helped to restrain the excesses of a capitalism that promotes the freedom of the powerful at the expense of human togetherness.

In 1991, soon after the collapse of Soviet-style communism, John Paul II reflected on the cold war in *Centesimus annus*. He notes the different ways in which communism was fought politically: either by "national security", so controlling the whole of society in order to make Marxist infiltration impossible, or in the "affluent society or the consumer society" to defeat Marxism on the level of pure materialism (CA, 19). Either way, the dignity of the human person suffered at the hands of political control or of economic greed. In the collapse of communism, almost entirely without violence, the victory of freedom over political and military might was in the Pope's understanding only possible through the virtue of solidarity: "the fall of this kind of 'bloc' or empire was accomplished almost everywhere by means of peaceful protest, using only the weapons of truth and justice" (CA, 23).

Solidarity thus expresses the commitment to human society and culture, that is to "the common good", but rooted in a deep respect for the value and the dignity of each human being. Solidarity recognizes the transcendence of the human being, whose heart can never be satisfied with material possessions alone: "there are collective and qualitative needs which cannot be satisfied by market mechanisms. There are important human needs which escape its logic. There are goods which by their very nature cannot and must not be bought or sold" (CA, 40).

The Eucharist and solidarity

The kingdom of God preached and inaugurated by Jesus Christ is the fulfilment of human solidarity. In the kingdom, each person will know her/his own dignity in right relationship to all other people. In the kingdom, there will be the full flowering of all persons and of all peoples. But the kingdom of God is not just a nebulous and beautiful idea that is found in the Bible. It is a reality that is already present on earth through the resurrection of Jesus and the sending of the Holy Spirit. Moreover, as John Paul II has said: "The Kingdom of God becomes present above all in the celebration of the sacrament of the Eucharist, which is the Lord's Sacrifice" (SRS, 48).

The Eucharist should therefore be the school in which we learn the virtue of solidarity. Each Eucharist is an expression of the Church. At Sunday Mass in our parishes, we do not choose our fellow worshippers. They include young and old, mobile and less mobile, affluent and needy. More and more, we find our congregations are inter-racial, made up of people from many lands. The Church at Mass is a microcosm of the kingdom, to which God calls people of every colour, race, tribe and nation. "The Sunday Eucharist which every week gathers Christians together as God's family round the table of the Word and the Bread of Life, is also the most natural antidote to dispersion. It is the privileged place where communion is ceaselessly proclaimed and nurtured" (NMI, 36).

In the Eucharist, this conglomeration of very different people is formed into one body through the gift of the one body. "Because there is one bread, we who are many are one body, for we all partake of the one bread" (1 Cor. 10:17). The Eucharist is the food of solidarity. It shapes us in togetherness and interdependence. "Thus the Lord unites us with himself through the Eucharist - sacrament and sacrifice - and he unites us with himself and with one another by a bond stronger than any natural union; and thus united, he sends us into the whole world to bear witness, through faith and works, to God's love, preparing the coming of his Kingdom and anticipating it, though in the obscurity of the present time" (SRS, 48).

Lord, form us in solidarity through your Eucharist. "Grant that we, who are nourished by his body and blood, may be filled with his Holy Spirit, and become one body, one spirit in Christ" (Eucharistic Prayer III).

Sources for teaching on solidarity

Paul VI, *Populorum progressio* (1967), paras. 44, 48

John Paul II, *Redemptor hominis* (1979), para. 16

John Paul II, *Laborem exercens* (1981), para. 8

John Paul II, *Familiaris consortio* (1984), paras. 43, 48, 72

John Paul II, *Sollicitudo rei socialis* (1987), paras. 23, 26, 33, 38 – 40, 45 – 47

John Paul II, *Centesimus annus* (1991), para. 23, 41, 49 – 51

Questions for discussion

How is solidarity different from communist collectivism and from *laissez-faire* capitalism?

Is the Pope's idea of human solidarity out of touch with reality? If not, why not?

How does the Eucharist produce solidarity? How can our celebration of Mass do more to form the virtue of solidarity?

Chapter

10

The Church and human rights

Blessed John XXIII was the first Pope to draw up a list of human rights. At a time of great political tension and danger he wrote his last encyclical *Pacem in terris,* issued at Easter 1963. Twenty years previously, the 1942 Christmas message of Pius XII in the middle of World War II, entitled "The rights of man", had contained a section on "The dignity and rights of the human person". But John Paul II is the Pope, who has done the most to develop a comprehensive Christian teaching on the dignity of the human person, the right ordering of society, the role of the Church, and the defence of human rights. Earlier chapters treating other aspects of the dignity of the human person have made some mention of human rights. In this chapter we will present the biblical and theological foundations for human rights, followed by a short summary of human rights of different kinds and a note of where the Church's teaching can be found.

The foundation for human rights

Catholic moral teaching has long been anchored in "natural law", that is the moral requirements placed by God in all human beings through creation and knowable by human reason. Over the last twenty-five years, John Paul II has provided a stronger theological basis for the Church's moral teaching, showing how the moral requirements for all people grounded in creation are fulfilled and realized in the coming of God's Son in human flesh. This development has made the Church's social teaching more biblical, without endangering its universal character and application.

In his first encyclical *Redemptor hominis* (1979), John Paul II reflects on the teaching of Vatican II: "Christ the Lord, Christ the new Adam, in the very revelation of the mystery of the Father and of his love, fully reveals man to himself and brings to light his most high calling" (GS, 22, cited in RH, 8). That is to say, human dignity is based on being created "in the image of God" (Gen. 1: 27); but it is in the incarnation of the Son of God and the redemption he won that the destiny of humanity is revealed and human dignity is shown forth. "In Christ, and through Christ, God has revealed himself fully to mankind and has definitively drawn close to it; at the same time, in Christ and through Christ, man has acquired full awareness of his dignity, of the heights to which he is raised, of the surpassing worth of his own humanity, and of the meaning of his existence" (RH, 11).

While human rights have always attached to the dignity of the human person, they have become of acute importance for the future of humanity in this last century "of great calamities for man" (RH, 17). In the twentieth century arose horrendous forms of totalitarian rule, under which the Holy Father himself suffered. Out of this experience, the Pope says: "The root of modern totalitarianism is to be found in the denial of the transcendent dignity of the human person who, as the visible image of the invisible God, is ... by his very nature the subject of rights which no one may violate — no individual, group, class, nation or State" (CA, 44).

Back in 1979, the Pope saw the emergence of the United Nations Organisation and its Declaration of Human Rights as signs of hope (RH, 17). But words must be followed by deeds, as the Holy Father wrote in 1999: "Fifty years after the solemn proclamation of the Universal Declaration of Human Rights, many people are still subjected to the most degrading forms of exploitation and manipulation, which make them veritable slaves to those who are more powerful" (EA, 33). In his New Year's message for 2004 in the context of combating terrorism, John Paul II has insisted on the need for "international law", which "is now called to develop legal instruments provided with effective means for the prevention, monitoring and suppression of crime."

For the Church, the dignity of each person is seen in the context of the solidarity of human society willed by God. The rights of each person are necessary so that each one can be an integral part of human society. So in the Catholic understanding, human rights are not seen as just "me" and "my rights", but in terms of the rights of all within a human society. All human rights are inter-connected, because all have been created by God and all lead to our common destiny in the kingdom of God.

The following outline of specific kinds of human right can be seen as a summary of the teaching on the dignity of the human person covered in the earlier chapters on life, sexuality, the family, leisure, work and solidarity. In each sphere of human life and interaction, the dignity of the human person calls for certain rights to be respected and upheld.

The right to life

The most fundamental right is the right to life of every innocent human being. All other rights depend upon this right. "Upon the recognition of this right, every human community and the political community itself are founded" (EV, 2). This right to life is not dependent on any other factors – health, age, race, education. "As far as the right to life is concerned, every innocent human being is absolutely equal to all others" (EV, 57).

In Chapter II of *Evangelium vitae,* the Pope talks of the positive Christian teaching concerning human life and its dignity: of the dignity of the unborn child (paras. 44 – 45), and of life in old age and human suffering (paras. 46 – 47). Then in Chapter III, he speaks of grave sins against human life: the "unspeakable crime of abortion" (paras. 58 – 63), the "tragedy of euthanasia" (paras. 64 – 67). Any appeal to human rights that denies that God is the Lord of life, such as the claims that a pregnant woman has a right to decide about the fruit of her own body, or that a terminally ill patient has a right to voluntary euthanasia, is illegitimate and without moral foundation.

In the Church's traditional teaching on a "just war", it was never morally permissible to target non-combatants. This is one reason why John Paul II has insisted that "acts of terrorism are never justifiable" (SRS, 24).

Rights concerning the family

In second place of importance come human rights concerning the family. The formation of the family preceded the formation of any nation, thus showing the centrality of the family in God's plan for human society.

"God is love and in Himself he lives a mystery of personal loving communion. Love is ... the fundamental and innate vocation of every human being" (FC, 11). This call to love is realized in one of two ways: marriage or celibacy. Either calling expresses "the most profound truth of man, of his being created 'in the image of God' " (FC, 11). For this reason, there is a human right to choose one's basic state in life.

The Pope deals with the rights of women (para. 22), the rights of children (para. 26) and the rights of parents regarding education (para. 36). FC summarizes the human rights concerning the family, that include: the right of every human being, even if he or she is poor, to found a family and to have adequate means to support it; the right to bring up children in accordance with the family's own traditions and religious and cultural values; the right to housing suitable for living family life in a proper way; the right to emigrate as a family in search of a better life (FC, 46).

A scale of human rights

While every human right is truly a right, demanding recognition and responsible behaviour, not all human rights have the same weight. The rights that are absolute concern what is most basic to human dignity (no abortion, no murder, no torture). Other rights are not all absolute, but depend on the directness of their connection with human dignity. For example, John Paul II repeats the teaching that there is a right to "private property", but says: "Christian tradition has never upheld this right as absolute and untouchable. On the contrary, it has always understood this right within the broader context of the right common to all to use the goods of the whole of creation: the right to private property is subordinated to the right to common use, to the fact that goods are meant for everyone" (LE, 14.2). The right to ownership belongs to the dignity of the human person, but this does not mean that there is a right to deprive others of their dignity.

Rights concerning the economy and employment

The Catholic Church has insisted on both the right and the duty to work, upholding also "the right to a just wage and to the personal security of the worker and his or her family" (LE, 8.6). The right to work, together with the right to a living wage, is linked to the right to support a family. There is also a right to rest and to holidays (LE, 19.6). There is a "right to a pension and to insurance for old age and in case of accidents at work" (LE 19, 6).

The Pope also speaks of "the right of economic initiative": "the denial of this right, or its limitation ... diminishes, or in practice absolutely destroys the spirit of initiative. ... In the place of creative initiative there appears passivity, dependence and submission to the bureaucratic apparatus" (SRS, 15). God has created us human beings to be able to think, to have ideas, to make decisions – not just for ourselves, but for our families, our local society and for the wider world.

Social, cultural and political rights

Among the human rights constantly upheld by the Pope is the right freely to associate with other people, another example of proper human initiative. So there is a"'natural human right' to form private associations" (CA, 7). This right is not dependent on the approval of public authorities.

Vatican II teaches that all people "of whatever race, condition or age, in virtue of their dignity as human persons, have an inalienable right to education" (GE, 1). "All Christians have a right to Christian education" (GE, 2). "Parents, who have a primary and inalienable duty and right in regard to the education of their children, should enjoy the fullest liberty in their choice of school" (GE, 6).

As patterns of human behaviour change and new forms of abuse arise, the upholding of the dignity of the human person requires a fresh formulation of human rights. So the problem of media intrusiveness has led one of the most recent Vatican documents to speak of "the right of privacy" (EE, 63).

The rights of nations

Rights do not just belong to individual persons, but also to groups and to nations. Nations have rights in relation to other nations. The Holy Father had long experience of the oppression of Poland by its more powerful neighbour to the East. It was enlightened by that experience that he says, "It often happens that a nation is deprived of … the "sovereignty" which is its right, in its economic, political-social and in a certain way cultural significance" (SRS, 15), and that he speaks of "the right of every people to its own identity, independence and security" (SRS, 21). A later document speaks of the need for "respect for diverse cultures to avoid their disappearance within the majority" (EE, 63).

The right to religious freedom

The subject of religious liberty warranted an entire document of Vatican II, the declaration *Dignitatis humanae*. This declaration had two main thrusts: first the affirmation that "the human person has a right to religious freedom" (DH, 2). This is based on the dignity of the human person who is to respond freely to the invitation of God and who is not to be coerced: "man's response to God by faith ought to be free, and that nobody is to be forced to embrace the faith against his will" (DH, 10). Secondly, religious communities have a right to free exercise of their faith that the State has no right to suppress: "provided the just requirements of public order are not violated, these groups [religious communities] have a right to immunity so that they may organize themselves according to their own principles" (DH, 4).

The Holy Father has always seen the right to religious freedom as the foundation for the free exercise of all other rights. The Pope after listing a series of human rights concludes: "In a certain sense, the source and synthesis of these rights is religious freedom, understood as the right to live in the truth of one's faith and in conformity with one's transcendent dignity as a person" (CA, 47). "The apex of development is the exercise of the right and duty to seek God, to know him and to live in accordance with that knowledge" (CA, 29). This is the message of Jesus: "You shall love the Lord your God with all your heart, and with all your soul, and with all your strength, and with all your mind; and your neighbour as yourself" (Luke 10:27).

Sources for teaching on human rights

Bl. John XXIII *Pacem in terris* (1963)

John Paul II *Familiaris consortio* (1981), para. 46

John Paul II *Sollicitudo rei socialis* (1987), paras. 6-9, 11, 15, 21, 26, 32-33, 46

John Paul II *Centesimus annus* (1991), paras. 6-9, 15-16, 22-24, 29, 47

John Paul II *Evangelium vitae* (1995), paras. 2, 57

John Paul II *Ecclesia in Asia* (1999) para. 33

John Paul II, *Ecclesia in Europa* (2003), para. 63

Questions for discussion

What is meant by a human right?

From whom can we claim human rights?

Show how different human rights are inter-connected, and discuss why some human rights are more foundational than others.

Why is the right to religious freedom a source and a support for all other human rights?

Chapter 11

The dignity of
the kingdom

As has been noted, the basis for the dignity of the human person in the Church's social teaching has moved from natural law to a more biblical view that grounds this dignity in creation but sees the full dignity of the human person most fully embodied in Jesus Christ. However, a fully biblical view of the human person also requires the future dimension of the kingdom of God that is still to come in all its fullness. Among the recent documents of the magisterium, it is the *Catechism of the Catholic Church* that has restored the coming kingdom to its proper biblical place in Catholic teaching. The eschatological hope of the Church was of course treated at Vatican II in the Constitution on the Church (LG, Chapter VII) and in the Constitution on the Church in the Modern World (GS, 39, 45), but in this area the Catechism teaching is fuller and richer than that in the Council documents.

So we now look at human dignity in the light of the coming of the kingdom of God. The dignity of the human person is conferred by God our Creator. This dignity comes both from our origin and from our destiny. "The dignity of the human person is rooted in his creation in the image and likeness of God; it is fulfilled in his vocation to divine beatitude" (CCC, 1700).

This citation begins the chapter in the Catechism on the dignity of the human person. It introduces the first two articles in this chapter, but we will look particularly at the second entitled "Our Vocation to Beatitude" (CCC, 1716 – 1729). Here the Catechism presents its teaching on the Beatitudes: "The Beatitudes reveal the goal of human existence, the ultimate end of human acts: God calls us to his own beatitude" (CCC, 1719). We are made for God. We are made to enjoy the fullness of life with God. We are called to "the banquet of life". So Jesus rewards those counted among the sheep at his right hand: "Come, O blessed of my Father, inherit the kingdom prepared for you from the foundation of the world" (Matt. 25:34).

The Beatitudes

This destiny of joy and righteousness in the kingdom of God is centred on Jesus Christ. We not only expect a kingdom, but also a king. It is this combination that prevents Christian teaching from degenerating into another ideology. What God promises is not just a new order of society, symbolized in the language of kingdom, but a society in which people are interiorly transformed by a Saviour. The promised reality of the coming kingdom already exists in a person, Jesus Christ. We do not just await the coming of the kingdom, but also the coming of the king, who embodies in his person all the qualities of the kingdom. So John Paul II speaks of Christian morality in this way: "More radically, it involves holding fast to the very person of Jesus, partaking of his life and of his destiny, sharing in his free and loving obedience to the will of the Father" (VS, 19).

The Beatitudes portray the way that Jesus lived and the horizons of his thinking. "The Beatitudes depict the countenance of Jesus Christ and portray his charity" (CCC, 1717). "In their originality and profundity they are a sort of self-portrait of Christ, and for this very reason are invitations to discipleship and to communion of life with Christ" (VS, 16).

The whole of life in Christ is directed towards the coming kingdom. There are nine beatitudes in the Sermon on the Mount in Matthew 5; seven of them speak of future blessings – the blessed shall be comforted, shall inherit the earth, shall be satisfied, shall obtain mercy, shall see God, shall be called sons of God, and their reward is great in heaven. We should notice how Jewish the beatitudes are: there is no separation between the personal and the social, no gap between the earthly and the heavenly. The comfort promised is not just individual solace – "Comfort, comfort my people, says your God" (Is. 40:1). The satisfied are not contented consumers but "those who hunger and thirst for righteousness" (Matt. 5:6). The sons of God are the peacemakers (Matt. 5: 9).

Already present,
but not yet fully manifest

The other two beatitudes end with the statement: "For theirs is the kingdom of heaven" (Matt. 5:3, 10). Here we encounter this twofold aspect of the teaching of Jesus on the kingdom. The kingdom of God is already present – through the coming of Jesus and the sending of his Spirit – but this hidden presence is a sign and a promise of the future coming of the kingdom in its visible fullness and glory.

Two categories of disciple are singled out as present bearers of the kingdom: the poor in spirit (Matt. 5:3) and those who are persecuted for the sake of righteousness (Matt. 5:9). It is important for us to relate human dignity to the poor and the oppressed. We are to recognize a dignity in the poor and oppressed: each one has a human face and a calling to the same destiny as ourselves. We are to treat the poor and the oppressed with dignity. "As you did it to one of the least of these my brethren, you did it to me" (Matt. 25:40).

Jesus the sign of our dignity

But to recognize Jesus in the poor and oppressed, we have to become disciples. We have to be healed ourselves from the wounds to human dignity caused by sin. Through sin, human dignity has been soiled and damaged. "The whole head is sick, and the whole heart faint. From the sole of the foot even to the head, there is no soundness in it, but bruises and sores and bleeding wounds" (Is. 1:5-6). Only through a Saviour can human dignity be restored. So Vatican II teaches: 'He who is the "image of the invisible God" (Col. 1:15), is himself the perfect man who has restored in the children of Adam that likeness to God which had been disfigured ever since the first sin" (GS, 22). Jesus is God's new beginning. He is the foundation of a new creation. St Paul says: "As in Adam all die, so also in Christ shall all be made alive" (1 Cor. 15:22). That is why the Fathers of the Church called Jesus "the new Adam" and the Church teaches: "Christ the new Adam, in the very revelation of the mystery of the Father and of his love, fully reveals man to himself and brings to light his most high calling" (GS, 22).

In Jesus Christ, then, we are presented with God's vision for humankind. He is true God who has become true man. In Jesus, human dignity is no longer just an ideal, it becomes a reality. "He worked with human hands, he thought with a human mind. He acted with a human will, and with a human heart he loved." (RH, 8). Jesus overcomes sin by suffering all the indignities that sinful man can heap upon him: "his appearance was so marred, beyond human semblance" (Is. 52:14); "he was despised, and we esteemed him not" (Is. 53:3). By the indignities he suffered, our dignity is restored: "by his wounds you have been healed" (1 Peter 2:24).

Human progress and the coming of the kingdom

The relationship between human society on earth and the coming "fully human" society of the kingdom of God is addressed most clearly in *Gaudium et spes*. "The form of this world, distorted by sin, is passing away and we are taught that God is preparing a new dwelling and a new earth in which righteousness dwells, whose happiness will fill and surpass all the desires of peace arising in the hearts of men" (GS, 39). The Church is a particular sign of the coming kingdom, through this hidden presence of the Lord, and is the chosen instrument for spreading the good news of the kingdom and hastening its full arrival. The Church "is to be a leaven and, as it were, the soul of human society in its renewal by Christ and transformation into the family of God" (GS, 40).

We all believe that as Christians we are being prepared by the Lord for the glory of heaven. But we easily think of this just in individual terms. This means, that we are being sanctified in this life and so are being prepared for death, through which we go to

God. But we know that when we die, we can take nothing with us. But this view only expresses one element in Christian faith. It overlooks the role of human society and of human culture. It forgets the promise of the resurrection on the last day and the vision of new heavens and a new earth (Is. 65:17; 66:22; 2 Peter 3:13). This raises the important question of the lasting value of our human achievements on earth: the value of our accumulated knowledge and technical skills, the value of human art, the value of human culture and civilization. While we cannot take these with us when we die, will they not in some way form part of the new world of the resurrection?

In *Gaudium et spes,* the Church did not attempt to answer all our questions. There is a recognition of what we do not know about the age to come. "We know neither the moment of the consummation of the earth and of man nor the way the universe will be transformed" (GS, 39). But in this same paragraph the Council did provide a framework in which to address these questions. On the one hand, earthly progress is not to be identified with the coming of the kingdom of God. Yet, nonetheless the growth of the human family on earth foreshadows in some way "the age which is to come" (GS, 39). Human progress is not irrelevant to the coming of the kingdom.

So the Church teaches that everything human is of value. But in this world, everything is still tainted in some way by the effects of sin. Nonetheless, everything that reflects the true dignity of man will find a place in the kingdom. But between the now of the Church in this world and the coming of the kingdom in its fullness, there will be death and resurrection. "The Church will enter the glory of the kingdom only through this final Passover, when she will follow her Lord in his death and resurrection" (CCC, 677). There will be a purification. "When we have spread on earth the fruits of our nature and our enterprise – human dignity, brotherly communion, and freedom - ... we will find them once again, cleansed this time from the stain of sin, illuminated and transfigured, when Christ presents to his Father an eternal and universal kingdom" (GS, 39).

The promotion of the dignity of the human person is then an intrinsic element in the Church's calling. It is essential to the preparation of the kingdom: "In pursuing its own salvific purpose not only does the Church communicate divine life to men but in a certain sense it casts the reflected light of that divine life over all the earth, notably in the way it heals and elevates the dignity of the human person, in the way it consolidates society, and endows the daily activity of men with a deeper sense and meaning" (GS, 40).

The centrality of the Church's liturgy

It is in the liturgy of the Church that the hope for God's future is most fully expressed and prepared. It is the liturgy that makes clear the personal and the communal character of the coming kingdom, which is there made present in sign form. It is the liturgy that holds before us the cosmic and universal character of the rule of Jesus, the Messiah of Israel.

This future dimension is present in every Mass, especially in the acclamations after the consecration, and in the "Deliver us" prayer that follows the Our Father. It is also present in Eucharistic Prayer, no. III. But it is especially in November and December each year that the "last days" are put before us. In November, the liturgy focuses on the last things: the coming of the Lord, the judgement, heaven and hell. This begins with the celebration of All Saints – those who have gone before us and now enjoy the vision of God – and of All Souls – praying for the souls of the faithful departed still in need of purification. The last week of the Church's year begins with the feast of Christ the King and then we move into the season of Advent, where the focus is on the coming king without the dark side.

The meaning of Advent

It is in Advent that the promises of the kingdom are consistently placed before us. The *Catechism* provides a wonderful description of the meaning of Advent. "When the Church celebrates the liturgy of Advent each year, she makes present this ancient expectancy of the Messiah, for by sharing in the long preparation for the Saviour's first coming, the faithful renew their ardent desire for his second coming" (para. 524). During Advent, we hear the wonderful promises in the Old Testament prophets about the coming of the Messiah-Saviour and of his kingdom.

In Advent, we are not playing games of pretence. We are not trying to put ourselves back in the centuries before Jesus came, and then suddenly on 25 December we discover again that he has come. No, we listen again to the Old Testament prophets to receive their longing for the fulfilment of all God's promises. When we hear that "He will swallow up death for ever, and the Lord God will wipe away tears from all faces" (Is. 25:8), we believe that in the resurrection of Jesus, death was swallowed up – for us; but we still await in hope our own resurrection and the destruction of death, "the last enemy" (1 Cor. 15:26). As we hear this promise, our faith and our longing for this final deliverance and restoration is rekindled and enlivened.

In the Old Testament promises of deliverance and salvation, there is a perfect harmony between the personal, the communal and the cosmic. The promises are of a Saviour-King, of a restored city and kingdom, and of a restored cosmos. God's vision for community and for society are anchored in a person. This is why Christian faith is neither just a philosophy nor an ideology. The coming kingdom that is promised will come about through all people and all things being brought into unity and conformity with Jesus. God's "plan for the fullness of time" is "to unite all things in him, things in heaven and things on earth" (Eph. 1:10).

As a liturgical season, Advent is a season of prayer and worship. In Advent, the Holy Spirit teaches the Church afresh how to pray for the coming of the Lord Jesus and his kingdom. The prayer of the Church is the prayer of the "time between" – between the first coming of the Lord and the second (see CCC, 1076).

The model for all Christian prayer is the Our Father. "It is the proper prayer of 'the end time,' the time of salvation that began with the outpouring of the Holy Spirit and will be fulfilled with the Lord's return" (CCC, 2771). In the risen Jesus, the coming kingdom has fully arrived, but in us it awaits its completion. We pray as those who have received the first fruits of the kingdom, the gift of the Holy Spirit, and as those who long for its fulfilment in the glory of the resurrection. The Catechism's teaching on prayer brings out this twofold aspect: "In prayer the disciple keeps watch, attentive to Him Who Is and Him Who Comes, in memory of his first coming in the lowliness of the flesh, and in the hope of his second coming in glory" (CCC, 2612).

In Advent the key word in the Church's prayer is "Come". Here again two biblical phrases resonate: "Come, Lord Jesus" (Rev. 22:20; see also 1 Cor. 16:22) and "Thy kingdom come" (Matt. 6:10; Luke 11:2). We cry out "Come" with confidence, because the kingdom is already established in Jesus himself. The divine blueprint is already complete. In Jesus the victory is won, the goal reached. He pours out his Holy Spirit to bring us to the same goal. We remember the first coming with faith, so that we can long for the second coming with hope. "Christ has died, Christ is risen, Christ will come again."

These two prayers "Come, Lord Jesus" and "Thy kingdom come" cover the whole plan of God and express the full hope of the Church. These prayers are expressing our longing for the day when all suffering and humiliation will be at an end. We long for the one kingdom in which the dignity of each person will be honoured, and our recreation in the image of God will be complete.

Sources for teaching on the coming kingdom

Second Vatican Council, *Lumen gentium,* 48-51

Second Vatican Council, *Gaudium et spes,* 39-40, 45

Catechism of the Catholic Church, 671-677, 769, 865, 1000-1002, 1040, 1107, 1130, 1403-1405, 2046, 2771-2772, 2816-2821

Questions for discussion

Why is the Christian hope more than going to heaven when we die?

Will the works of Leonardo da Vinci, Shakespeare, and Beethoven have a place in the coming Kingdom?

What is the difference between praying "Thy kingdom come" and praying "Come, Lord Jesus"?

Epilogue

The Dignity of Mary

It seems fitting to close this book on the dignity of the human person with a short reflection on the dignity of the woman chosen to bear the incarnate Son of God. It is fitting because it emphasizes once again that God's creative and redemptive work produces transformation in people and not just an inspiring theology. It is fitting because as a woman, Mary embodies human dignity in feminine form; this is especially important when we recall how women have played such a key role in upholding and defending the dignity of humans. It is fitting finally because Pope John Paul II has consistently exalted Mary as an illustration of human dignity and invoked her intercession for the protection and promotion of the dignity of all people.

The Dignity of the Maiden

In the story of the Annunciation, it is striking how the archangel Gabriel shows such great respect and reverence to the young maiden of Nazareth. It is perhaps part of Mary's puzzlement why she should be so greeted and honoured. The whole exchange between Gabriel and Mary is filled with a sense of grace and honour. As the Holy Father says "since Mary receives this 'new life' with a fullness corresponding to the Son's love for the Mother, and thus corresponding to the dignity of the divine motherhood, the angel at the Annunciation calls her 'full of grace'."(RM, 10). Dignity evokes dignity.

The dignity that God accords to humans is shown by the freedom and space God gives to Mary. God never treats human beings as mere instruments for the effecting of his purposes. God does not coerce. Mary is not commandeered. She is able to ask questions of the angel and receive an answer. God respects the human freedom he has created. It is with full liberty and total dignity that Mary replies in faith: "Behold, I am the handmaid of the Lord; let it be to me according to your word." (Luke 1: 38).

Dignity in Loving Service

The one New Testament episode where we catch a glimpse of Mary as servant of others comes in the story of the wedding feast in Cana. She seems to have known the families better than Jesus did, for her presence is described first and in a different way (see John 2: 1-2). When an embarrassing moment occurs, and the supply of wine runs out, Mary does two things. She informs Jesus " They have no wine" (John 2: 3). She does not beg, she trusts her son. Then she tells the servants to do what Jesus says. Mary is the one who takes the initiative to solve the problem. She acts decisively, but in a discreet way. She doesn't order the servants around. She quietly prepares the way for Jesus to perform his first sign.

Dignity in Suffering

We know that there must have been much suffering in Mary's life. The Catholic Church celebrates these liturgically with the commemoration of the Seven Sorrows of Mary on 15th September. She had to endure the unspoken reproach of Joseph before the angel enlightened him as to the cause of Mary's pregnancy. She could not tell him, but she could only trust God. Then there was the discomfort of travelling to Bethlehem with the baby's birth imminent. Again she had to trust Joseph when he obeys the command received in a dream " Rise, take the child and his mother, and flee to Egypt, and remain there till I tell you." (Matt. 2: 13). Another long journey, with an uncertain destination. Mary knew first-hand the sufferings and trials of a refugee having to flee from her own land and people.

It is above all at the foot of the cross that we see the dignity of Mary in her suffering. It is expressed above all in one word *"eistekeisan"* translated in Latin as "stabat", hence the hymn Stabat Mater: "The mother was standing." In the liturgy the Church applies to this moment of heart-rending grief the words of Lamentations: "Look and see if there is any sorrow like my sorrow" (Lam. 1: 12). She suffers the horror of her son's crucifixion with unflinching faith and fortitude. This is the supreme expression of the dignity of Mary.

Mother of the Living

Mary continues her quiet, profound and dignified presence. After the trauma of Calvary and the joy of the resurrection, she joins the apostles in the upper room, together with "the women" and "the brothers" of Jesus (Acts 1: 14). With them, she is devoting herself to prayer. The others know she stood at the foot of the cross. "By her complete adherence to the Father's will, to his Son's redemptive work, and to every prompting of the Holy Spirit, the Virgin Mary is the Church's model of faith and charity." (CCC, 967).

In *Evangelium vitae*, the Pope presents this model role of Mary in terms of her motherhood: "Mary is truly the Mother of God, the *Theotokos*, in whose motherhood the vocation to motherhood bestowed by God on every woman is raised to its highest level. Thus Mary becomes the model of the Church, called to be the 'new Eve', the mother of believers, the mother of the 'living' (Gen 3: 20)." (EV, 103).

The Battle Against Evil

In *Evangelium vitae*, John Paul II speaks of the two portents mentioned in Revelation 12: "the great portent....of the woman"(12: 1) and that of "a great red dragon" (12: 3), which "represents Satan, the personal power of evil" (EV, 104). The attack of the enemy is directed against motherhood and its fruits. " The dragon stood before the woman who was about to bear a child, that he might devour her child when she brought it forth" (Rev. 12: 4). Further on in this chapter, we are told: "And when the dragon saw that he had been thrown down to the earth, he pursued the woman who had borne the male child." (Rev. 12: 13) and "Then the dragon was angry with the woman, and went off to make war on the rest of her offspring, on those who keep the commandments of God and bear testimony to Jesus." (Rev. 12: 17).

While the woman in Revelation 12 clearly evokes first the maternal role of Israel and of Jerusalem and at the end the motherhood of the Church, it is wrong to exclude Mary from our exegesis. For Mary is the embodiment of Israel's call to bring forth the Saviour, and she is the embodiment of the Church that welcomes and proclaims him. So the Pope teaches: "Mary thus helps the Church to realize that life is always at the centre of a great struggle between good and evil, between light and darkness." (EV, 104).

It is fitting that this reflection on the dignity of the person ends with the reminder that in defending the dignity of human life we are not just dealing with good and bad choices, but with the age-long spiritual battle between light and darkness. As the apostle says: "For we are not contending against flesh and blood, but against the principalities, against the powers, against the world rulers of this present darkness, against the spiritual hosts of wickedness in the heavenly places." (Eph. 6: 12). To prevail in the struggle, the Christian must "take the whole armour of God" (Eph. 6: 13), that is composed of truth, the breastplate of righteousness, the gospel of peace, the shield of faith, the helmet of salvation, the sword of the Spirit that is the Word of God, and pray at all times in the Spirit (Eph. 6: 14-18). "Showing us the Son, the Church assures us that in him the forces of death have already been defeated: 'Death with life contended: combat strangely ended! Life's own champion, slain, yet lives to reign'." (EV, 105).

Glossary

The following are abbreviations cited in the text:

CA Encyclical Letter *Centesimus annus* of Pope John Paul II (1991)

CCC *Catechism of the Catholic Church* (1994)

CL Apostolic Exhortation *Christifideles laici* of Pope John Paul II (1988)

DD Apostolic Letter *Dies domini* of Pope John Paul II (1998)

DH Declaration *Dignitatis humanae* of the Second Vatican Council (1965)

EA Apostolic Exhortation *Ecclesia in Asia* of Pope John Paul II (1999)

EE Apostolic Exhortation *Ecclesia in Europa* of Pope John Paul II (2003)

ES Encyclical Letter *Ecclesiam suam* of Pope Paul VI (1964)

EV   Encyclical Letter *Evangelium vitae* of Pope John Paul II (1995)

FC   Apostolic Exhortation *Familiaris consortio* of Pope John Paul II (1981)

GE   Declaration *Gravissimum educationis* of the Second Vatican Council (1965)

GS   The Constitution *Gaudium et spes* of the Second Vatican Council (1965)

LE   Encyclical Letter *Laborem exercens* of Pope John Paul II (1981)

LF   Letter to Families of Pope John Paul II (1994)

LG   The Constitution *Lumen gentium* of the Second Vatican Council (1964)

MD   Apostolic Letter *Mulieris dignitatem* of Pope John Paul II (1988)

NMI   Apostolic Letter *Novo millennio ineunte* of Pope John Paul II (2001)

PP   Encyclical Letter *Populorum progressio* of Pope Paul VI (1967)

RH   Encyclical Letter *Redemptor hominis* of Pope John Paul II (1979)

RM   Encyclical Letter *Redemptoris mater* of Pope John Paul II (1987)

SC   The Constitution *Sacrosanctum concilium* of the Second Vatican Council (1963)

SRS   Encyclical Letter *Sollicitudo rei socialis* of Pope John Paul II (1987)

TB   *The Theology of the Body:Human Love in the Divine Plan*, by Pope John Paul II (1997)

UUS   Encyclical Letter *Ut unum sint* of Pope John Paul II (1995)

VS   Encyclical Letter *Veritatis splendor* of Pope John Paul II (1993)